Number Twelve

Carolyn and Ernest Fay Series in Analytical Psychology

David H. Rosen, General Editor

The Carolyn and Ernest Fay edited book series, based initially on the annual Fay Lecture Series in Analytical Psychology, was established to further the ideas of C. G. Jung among students, faculty, therapists, and other citizens and to enhance scholarly activities related to analytical psychology. The Book Series and Lecture Series address topics of importance to the individual and to society. Both series were generously endowed by Carolyn Grant Fay, the founding president of the C. G. Jung Educational Center in Houston, Texas. The series are in part a memorial to her late husband, Ernest Bel Fay. Carolyn Fay has planted a Jungian tree carrying both her name and that of her late husband, which will bear fruitful ideas and stimulate creative works from this time forward. Texas A&M University and all those who come in contact with the growing Fay Jungian tree are extremely grateful to Carolyn Grant Fay for what she has done. The holder of the McMillan Professorship in Analytical Psychology at Texas A&M functions as the general editor of the Fay Book Series.

Memories of Our Lost Hands

Memories
of Our Lost Hands

Searching for
Feminine Spirituality
and Creativity

SONOKO TOYODA

Texas A&M University Press   College Station

The paper used in this book meets the minimum requirements
of the American National Standard for Permanence
of Paper for Printed Library Materials, z39.48–1984.
Binding materials have been chosen for durability.

∞

Library of Congress Cataloging-in-Publication Data

Toyoda, Sonoko.
  Memories of our lost hands : searching for feminine spirituality
and creativity / Sonoko Toyoda.
      p. cm.—(Carolyn and Ernest Fay series in analytical
psychology ; no. 12)
  Includes bibliographical references and index.
  ISBN 1-58544-435-9 (cloth : alk. paper)
  1. Hand—Religious aspects.   2. Women—Religious life.
3. Women—Psychology.   4. Creative ability.   I. Title.   II. Series.
  BL325.H23T69 2006
  155.3'33—dc22   2005022829

For my mother
and my daughter

ঽ

Contents

Foreword

DAVID H. ROSEN

Where the spirit does not work with the hand, there
is no art.

— Leonardo da Vinci

At first I wondered, how could Sonoko Toyoda do it, that is, give four
lectures and write a whole book on hands? Not only has she done
it, but this remarkable book—an artistic product from her creative
imagination—is crucial for both women and men (through the
anima). Toyoda has found her own lost hands, and by actualizing
her feminine spirituality and creativity she models this process for
others.

This is an invigorating book about feminine hands (representing
the heart) overthrowing the dominance of masculine hands (representing the head). It reminds me of Carl Jung's visit to the Taos pueblo
in New Mexico, where he befriended Chief Ochwiay Biano (Mountain
Lake). Mountain Lake thought that white people looked cruel, always
wanted something, and seemed uneasy, restless, and mad. When Jung
asked him why he thought the whites were like this, Mountain Lake
replied, "They say that they think with their heads." Jung said, "Why,
of course," and he asked him in surprise, "What do you think with?"
Mountain Lake indicated his heart.[1]

Toyoda helps us recognize and develop our left side of the heart—
the feminine side, but her focus is on the hands. The left hand is connected to the right brain (the seat of maternal feelings and healing
images). Leonard Shlain points out that "Women have more rods in

their retinas than men and, as a result, have better peripheral union. They can see better in the dark." He also states, "The left hand is more protective than the right and is the one that commonly holds a baby." In Western culture the left hand has taken on connotations of things sinister, wrong, dark, and evil (paralleling what happened to women as they were oppressed by men). Like Toyoda, Shlain emphasizes the need for more of the feminine to balance the masculine in every person. Toyoda adds the rich, dark, archetypal, feminine *yin* of the East to help balance the overdeveloped, light, masculine *yang* of the West. She helps us see and accept the necessity of a "visible darkness," as outlined by Junichiro Tanizaki. He challenges us to "immerse ourselves in the darkness and there discover its own particular beauty." Additionally, he urges us "to comprehend the mystery of shadows," upon which Toyoda elaborates.[2] We need to overcome our fear of the dark, reconnect with our lost hands, and actualize our feminine spirituality and creativity.

From an Eastern perspective, Toyoda illuminates the feminine, just as Irene de Castillejo does from a Western viewpoint. However, by concentrating on the hands, which Toyoda feels are the key to climbing out of the dark manhole and finding the light of day, she goes much farther. She encourages women to stand up for a feminine point of view and to do so with backbone! She reveals that women can handle the challenge and no longer have to feel or be handicapped in a patriarchal world. In its own way, Toyoda's work is as important as Clarissa Pinkola Estés's classic book, *Women Who Run with the Wolves*.[3] However, Toyoda considers the hands as both a converging point and the hope for not only women (and men) but also for Mother Earth and our global village.

Joan Erikson, who spotlights a ninth and final stage of life (which circles back and is similar to the first stage of life) beyond Erik Erikson's eight stages of psychosocial development, wisely states, "Hands, understanding, capable, talented hands. . . . Conscious and attentive use of the hands would make all our lives more meaningful. . . . Hands are essential for vital involvement in living."[4]

In her introduction, Toyoda primes us for seeing hands as having their own wisdom, one truly connected to the heart and soul, as well as being necessary for the development of feminine spirituality and creativity in both women and men.

The first chapter reviews the Grimm brothers' fairytale "The Handless Maiden," noting that the same basic story also exists in traditional Japanese fairytales. Toyoda shows how "The Handless Maiden" is extremely relevant to those modern women who feel they lack spirituality and creativity. She stresses that men cannot return to women what they took from them during the centuries of male domination. Women must recover it on their own.

In chapter two, "Hands as a Symbol of Feminine Creativity," Toyoda uses the hands of the sculptor Camille Claudel and the painter Frida Kahlo to powerfully illustrate her thesis. She asserts that, for women (and men), the feminine spirit is required for creativity. I agree with her position and that the muse (which is always feminine) must be present, both in women and men, for creativity to emerge and result in a work of art.

In her third chapter, "Hands as the Symbol of Feminine Spirituality," Toyoda introduces us to the feminine origins of Japanese spirituality, which is tied to nature and deeply rooted in the Earth. She also underscores that, in Japan, people join their hands together to pray, just as they do in most other countries. In addition, Toyoda discusses the Black Virgin of the West, linking her to the ancient dark Mother Earth Goddess as well as the dark feminine enigma of the East. Toyoda describes pilgrimages to Black Virgins around the world, discussing the ones in Japan (Kannon worship) in detail. She tells of the Senju Kannon with its thousand hands. As Toyoda states, all of these hands "represent the mercy to save everyone by any and all means." She maintains that these outer pilgrimages need to become inner ones that lead to creative activities accomplished with a woman's own hands, thereby restoring her feminine spirituality. Toyoda says, "The hand is used to express something that is springing up from deep within oneself."

In chapter four, "How to Recover Our Lost Hands," Toyoda outlines "what to do." Jungian psychotherapy and analysis, with its active imagination and resultant artistic products (poems, paintings, dances, sculptures, etc.), are high on the list for restoring feminine spirituality. She discusses the applicability of the wild-woman arche-type, as described by Clarissa Pinkola Estés, to the natural integration of a woman's creativity with her spirituality. Toyoda also discusses "obstacles to feminine creativity," "abandonment of creativity," "the problem of being a victim," and "hands receiving God's will." This chapter is informative, inspiring, and practical.

The last chapter ends with a summary of how to recover one's fem-inine spirituality by using one's hands creatively. Utilizing a brother-sister archetype, Toyoda emphasizes the equality of a woman and man. In addition, she stresses the need to accept the dark and frightful aspects of oneself as well as the bright and favorable. Finally, she al-lows a series of drawings, based on a dream by a young woman artist, to tell the story. This book is an extremely important work that is sure to take root around the world and to help us integrate and balance female and male, East and West.

Notes

1. David Rosen, *The Tao of Jung: The Way of Integrity* (New York: Penguin, 1997), p. 93.

2. Leonard Shlain, *The Alphabet versus the Goddess: The Conflict between Word and Image* (New York: Viking Penguin, 1998), pp. 26–27; Junichiro Tanizaki, *In Praise of Shadows* (New Haven, Conn.: Leete's Island Books, 1977), pp. 35, 31, 18. Trans. Thomas J. Harper and Edward G. Seiden-sticker.

3. Irene C. de Castillejo, *Knowing Woman: A Feminine Psychology* (New York: Harper, 1974); Clarissa Pinkola Estés, *Women Who Run with the Wolves* (New York: Ballantine, 1992).

4. Erik H. Erikson and Joan M. Erikson, *The Life Cycle Completed* (New York: W. W. Morton, 1998), pp. 120–21. Extended version by Joan M. Erikson with a new chapter on the ninth stage of development.

Acknowledgments

Totally unexpected things sometimes happen in life. For example, I never imagined that I would one day be invited to speak at the Carolyn and Ernest Fay Lecture Series. When David H. Rosen first suggested that I accept the invitation, I thought he was joking. However, when I attended Clarissa Estés's lectures in New Harmony, Indiana, for the Tenth Fay Lecture Series, I realized he was serious. At that time, Estés joined Rosen in persuading me. She said solemnly, "You should do it. It is not for your honor, but it is your obligation." Even after hearing her words of encouragement, the offer still seemed to be too big a challenge. I felt intimidated and scared.

Four months later, Rosen sent me an e-mail asking for my answer. On the same day, I also received a warm e-mail from Estés. By chance, both of these arrived on my birthday. This coincidence was enough to convince me to accept the invitation. I tell this story because many women today are frightened of taking a step into the unknown. Indeed, I wrote this book as a way of overcoming my own timidity. It will please me greatly if this book encourages women who are hesitant to take risks in their lives, and it is my sincere hope that this book will help them, as it has me, to reflect upon themselves.

First of all, I would like to express my gratitude to Carolyn Fay, who afforded me an opportunity to present my ideas in the warm atmosphere of the Fay Lecture Series. The accepting and cordial environment there is a result of Fay's presence and personality. I am also very grateful to David Rosen, who spared no effort in helping me prepare for the lecture. He edited my presentation and also wrote an excellent foreword for this book. In addition, I am indebted to Clarissa Estés, without whose encouragement I would not have accepted the offer to participate in the series. Moreover, she attended my lectures and encouraged me in her wonderfully sensitive way like a guardian angel. I would also like to thank the kind audience who persevered with me as I struggled with the English language.

I wish to express my special thanks to Lisa Gayle Bond, who not only translated my manuscript into English but also encouraged me to continue my work. Moreover, I appreciate the cooperation of those who have given me permission to use their drawings, photographs, and dream materials to illustrate this book. Many of my ideas were conceived in encounters with my analysands, to whom I am also very grateful. This book is a continuation of the thoughts that are expressed in my thesis, which was submitted to the C. G. Jung Institute in Zurich in 1992. I thank Catherine Moreau, who was my analyst in Zurich and who endorsed my ideas when they were still in their infancy.

Finally, I deeply appreciate the efforts of the editorial staff at Texas A&M University Press. I am especially grateful to Diana Vance and Stephanie George. Since my written English is less than fully fluent and I am unfamiliar with the conventions of American publishing, I am certain they have had to spend extra time getting this manuscript ready for publication.

This book seems like a small wonder in the sense that it could not have been realized without the help of so many people—and their warm hands. I humbly thank them all.

*Color Plates 1–9 constitute a series of drawings and words by
Mari Watanabe. Displayed at an exhibition of works by graduates of
Tama Art University in March, 2002, at Yokohama City Gallery.
Reproduction in this book is courtesy of Mari Watanabe.*

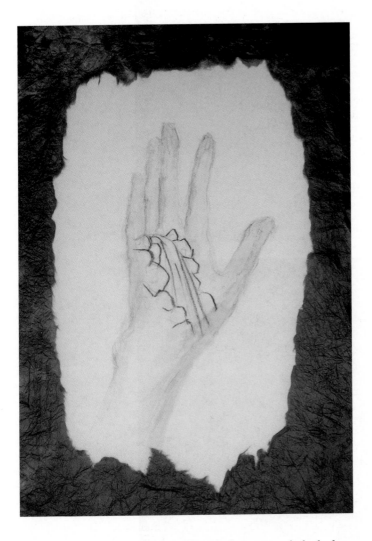

*Plate 1. "One day I had a dream where I had a tattoo on the back of
my hand. An image of a waterfall was tattooed."*

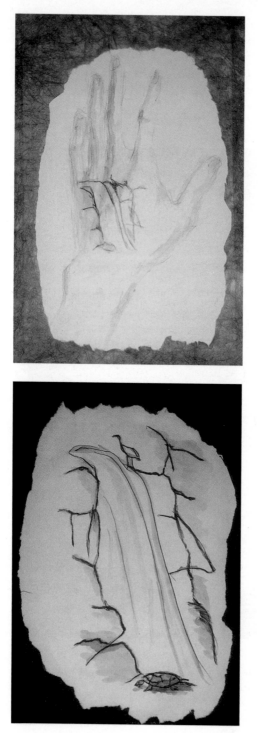

Plate 2. "Suddenly the tattooed image of the waterfall
began to move. It became
a real waterfall, and its
water turned into blood
and began to flow in my
blood vessel—flow and flow
abundantly."

Plate 3.

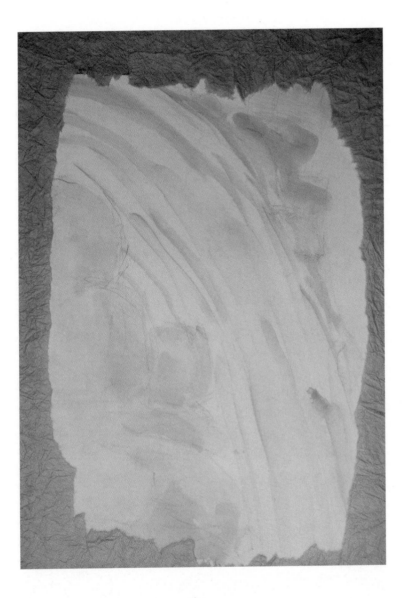

Plate 4.

Plate 5.

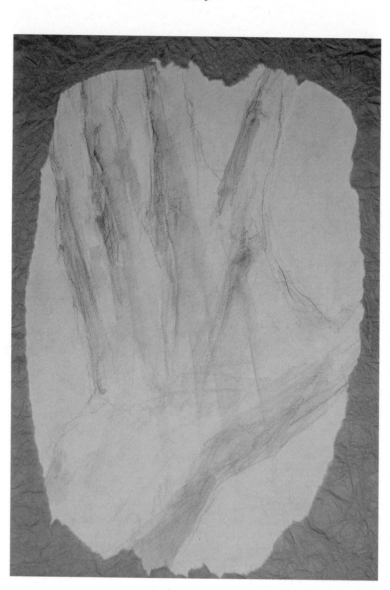

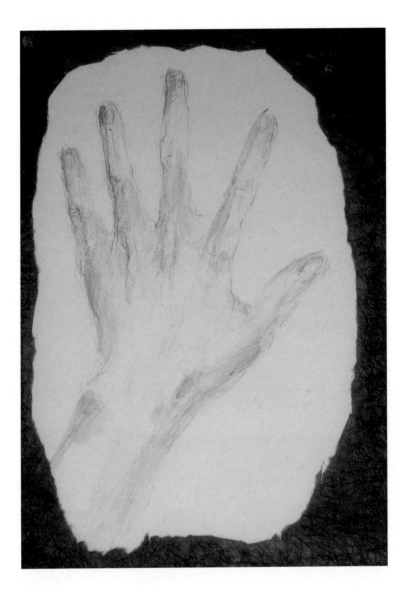

Plate 6. "And the hand tried to grasp something."

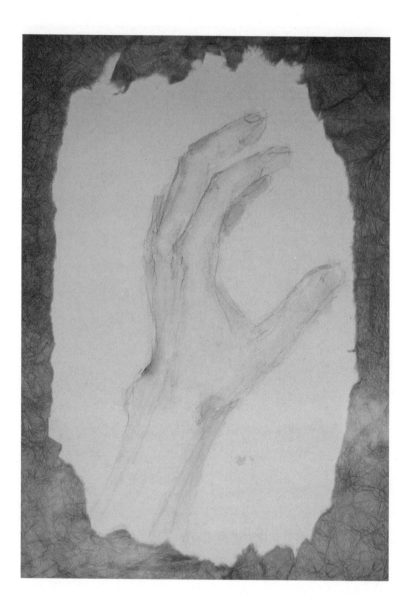

Plate 7.

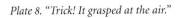
Plate 8. "Trick! It grasped at the air."

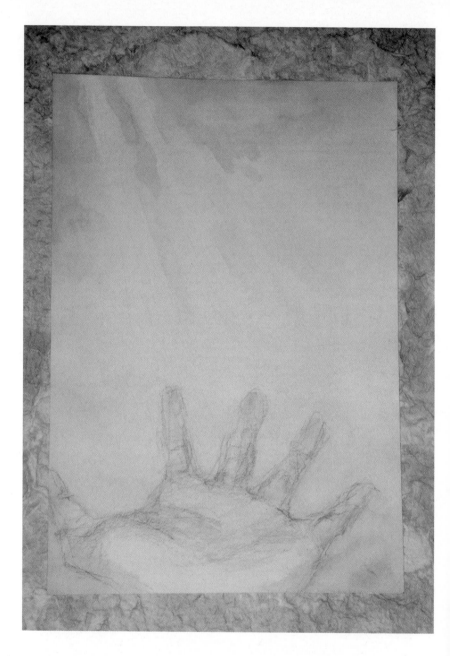

Plate 9. "And, when it opened again, there I found bright light and hope."

Memories of Our Lost Hands

Introduction

Often the hands know how to solve a riddle that the
intellect has wrestled with in vain.

—C. G. Jung

The human hand is the one thing that separates us from other animals. Humans stand upright and walk on two legs, and they are able to use their hands freely. Of course other primates have hands, but theirs have not developed to the same degree as ours. Human hands can make fires, create tools, and use those tools to do countless things. Unlike other animals, we have been helped by our hands to move toward civilization. Certainly we can also say that a prime reason for this lies in the development of the human brain, which directs the hands' movements. However, haven't we all experienced the way that our hands sometimes seem to move before they receive direction from our brain?[1] We might then consider the possibility that the human brain has been able to develop to such a high degree *because* humans have hands and have been able to use them.

Descartes said, "I think, therefore I am."[2] In his dualistic philosophy of mind and body, he declared the superiority of the human mind over the body. With this idea, the possibility of the body's thinking was subsequently rejected. Even so, a large number of artists and master artisans recognize the autonomous movement of their hands. Hands are not merely tools that work only under the brain's directives. Yet, many of us who have studied this dualistic perspective regard the body as something that is subordinated to the mind, and we have only the slightest inclination to learn from the body. In some ways we have lost or forgotten the wisdom and gifts of the body, as often expressed through the hands.

Along with Descartes' philosophy developed the rationalism of modern times; thus the development of scientific innovation took off at a rapid pace. Thanks to that, we are now reaping its benefits. Unfortunately, the radical developments of this scientific evolution have resulted in the destruction of our natural environment as evidenced by global warming, and we are standing on somewhat shaky ground today. Scientific progress has developed so quickly that we humans have at some point forgotten that we are an integral part of nature. For this reason we now need to stop for a while and reconsider the fact that human beings cannot be deciphered only by a reasoning brain. I think that it is thus necessary that we once again reflect on the meaning of our hands. Of course, hands are part of our bodies, and yet they seem to be wiser than any other part except for the brain. It might be important for us to consider that our hands "connect" our minds and bodies.

Hands produce things. However, their function is not simply to make things. Humans have been able to live through the ages because our hands have been able to gather food to sustain our bodies. In this sense, it is apparent that the hands are vital to human life. With our hands we are able to pick up and hold things, and the sense of touch that comes from our hands helps us to discern things. Hands are antennae—secondary eyes. They connect one person with another. With their hands, people are able to take care of one another, love one another, and heal one another. When people attack others or protect themselves, they use their hands. Hands can express human emotions. Sometimes our hands convey more than facial expressions do. And we mustn't forget that hands are used when we pray. In most of the world's religions, people put their hands together when they pray. Obviously hands are truly connected to our hearts and souls.

I have considered hands from various angles, but what I would most like to do is to consider hands as a symbol of feminine spirituality. By feminine spirituality I refer to what was lost in the dualistic idea that arose in rationalism. It is also what was almost eradicated during the ferocious witch-hunting of Descartes' era. It is well known that the women who were accused of being witches and burned at the stake were so-called wise women who inherited feminine wisdom. For instance, they were often women who had knowledge of midwifery and various homeopathic or natural herbs and medicines.[3] Some of these women perhaps had an intuitive ability to prophesy the future. Such feminine wisdom seems to be something that is passed on from woman to woman. It might be a sort of "groundwater" that is transmitted from a mother to a daughter, a kind of intuitive insight, or a type of transcendent wisdom beyond rational thinking. I perceive this type of wisdom not as intellectual in nature but rather something that is connected to the body and that in turn connects women to nature. From a rational point of view, this feminine quality seems unfathomable, mysterious, and uncanny. Small wonder, then, that men with a rational mind felt threatened by it. Perhaps the excessive deviation of the witch-hunting derived from men's tremendous fear of feminine power. Although Christianity eventually spread all across Europe, in days gone by, pre-Christian female wisdom and knowledge had great import for the general public.

One of the most important images of female spirituality is Sophia, and many pre-Christian Mother Earth goddesses with various special attributes also come to mind. There are Isis and Ishtar, who possess a fearful power over life and death and can travel between heaven and the underworld. Likewise, the horrible image of Medusa is one that we all know; however, not many of us realize that she was originally a goddess of wisdom. It is said that Athena turned Medusa into a terrifying, snake-haired monster because she envied Medusa's beauty. The power of her eyes—whose stare could turn her victims into stone—is evidence of her penetrating wisdom, and thus she frightens humans. In Christianity, the Virgin Mary represents feminine spirituality. However, in her case, the very powerful and frightening elements are removed. Only in the cult of the Black Virgin do we still see traces of the original image of feminine spirituality.[4]

Witch-hunting and the religious revolution brought about the rejection of femininity, while the rationalists established their authority through the use of language. Consequently, masculine values began to influence the way people thought and acted. Unfortunately, this also caused female spirituality to fade in prominence. People began to devalue the spiritual side of females, and the transmitting of feminine spiritual qualities from mother to daughter diminished and in some cases even ceased entirely. Women began to forget the gifts that their mothers and predecessors had possessed, and in their place, men's values and ideas began to shape women's thoughts and behavior.

Although I have discussed this phenomenon so far from a Western, historical point of view, it is apparent to a greater or lesser degree in every civilized country today. In the East, particularly in Japan, a witch-hunting period per se has never occurred. Moreover, within Japanese culture, feminine spirituality remains very deeply ingrained in the aesthetic sense. Yet, from the Middle Ages on, males have controlled Japanese cultural trends. Beginning in the sixth century, with the introduction of Buddhism into Japan and because of the influence of its teachings, women became secondary members of society, and their original power began to ebb. They were considered to be impure; therefore, certain rules and restrictions were applied to them. Nevertheless, in Japanese mythology, Amaterasu, the female sun goddess, is at the top of the Japanese pantheon. However, upon a closer examination of Japanese myths, one realizes that Amaterasu has no actual powers. Instead, the real power lies in a paternal god-figure behind her, and it is this god that influences Amaterasu's actions. Like the Greek goddess Athena, Amaterasu is a typical father's daughter, born from her father's eye. However, by placing Amaterasu at the top of the pantheon, Japanese culture preserves the feminine spiritual traits, at least in an aesthetic and symbolic sense.

As in the West, people's view—and their fear—of feminine power is personified by witches; in Japan, a similar embodiment would be an old woman called Yamanba, who lives deep in the mountains and is sometimes depicted as an ogress. She resembles Babayaga, the old crone who, in Russian fairytales, lives in the forest. These women are not simply frightening characters; they actually help damsels in distress in the stories. In Noh theater—a Japanese mask play that traces its roots to the fourteenth century—women's resentment or repressed grudge has been expressed as a female ghost or spirit and represents an important theme. The Noh actor who plays this ghost wears a mask signifying the fearful ogress called Hannya, who is reminiscent of Medusa. Hannya, which comes from the Sanskrit word *prajña,* means "transcendent and ultimate wisdom." Unfortunately, this meaning is not well known or understood by the Japanese people, who see Hannya only as a menacing entity. Medusa, too, is known more for her frightening face than for her wisdom. In other words, both in the West and in Japan, female wisdom has taken on a connotation of frightfulness, and this image has become well accepted by people at the conscious level. From another point of view, one could say that people are so fearful of feminine wisdom that they have imposed a terrifying image on it and avoided it. Unfortunately, women's wisdom has been viewed so negatively over the years that it is now deeply buried. In Noh theater, the feminine spirits or ogresses are commonly driven away by a male shaman or an exorcist, and Noh theater itself appears to be a symbolic ritual to drive away the feminine spirit.

My interest in feminine spirituality comes from my analytical practice as well as from my reflections on myself. Many of the women I have encountered in my practice have made me realize that numerous problems are seemingly caused by a lack of feminine spirituality. Women, without even knowing it, tend to evaluate themselves through men's eyes, and not a few women are betraying their feminine souls by doing so. Through the analytical process, many women have begun to recognize that they are extremely influenced by the male value system. With this recognition, they begin to peel the layers away one by one—the layers of the male value system that they have inflicted upon themselves. However, after doing so, they sometimes find nothing but a black void in the place where they should find their feminine self or a certain feminine core. One analysand in her forties had a recurrent dream of going through her home looking for something. She did not know what she was looking for; all she knew was that she was searching for something.

What is missing? I believe that the missing core of the female might be feminine spirituality. When women have adapted too much to the male value system, they even forget where they have put the feminine self. I think in order for women to see themselves as what they truly are, they must look deep within themselves and search for that buried aspect of female spirituality in the depth of their psyche. In order for women to be able to stand on their own two feet and protect and honor themselves as women, this is vital.

The analysand who had a recurrent dream of looking for something in her house one day had another searching dream, but in that vision she finally encountered someone in one of the rooms. After that, she had no further searching dreams. Who was the person she met in the dream? Her deceased grandmother. The grandmother had a very strong personality, and my analysand said that that was why she had been very critical of her grandmother while the woman was alive. However, through this dream this woman realized that her criticism was based on a male value system and furthermore that she needed to adopt the strength that her grandmother had possessed in order to stand upon her own two feet.

Over a long span of time within the male-oriented logos world, it has been very difficult to find words that can truly explain or define female spirituality. For this reason I began to search for something that could symbolize female spirituality. I once considered "salt" as such a symbol. Salt not only rules the very life force of humankind— our bodily fluids contain salt—but it is also a symbol of wisdom.[5] In this book I discuss hands as another symbol of feminine spirituality.

Most objects result from the work of hands; thus hands have a truly creative nature. As I consider them to be a symbol of feminine spirituality, I also view them as representing the creative aspects of women. I believe that these two are somehow connected. As women today begin to search for the feminine spiritual aspect that has been lost over time and attempt to recapture it, I believe they also need to examine their creative side. Through recovery of their female spirituality as well as their creativity, they will once again be able to respect and have faith in themselves—qualities that are irreplaceable and that no one else can bestow upon them.

For this reason, I would like mainly for women to consider my ideas. Nevertheless, we all need to remember that the withering away of feminine spirituality is not just a women's issue. If the modern ego was established in return for a hero's symbolic conquest of a dragon, feminine spirituality is also cut up and thrown away or subjugated to such a point that it cannot be found at all; all of humankind needs to recall that we are a part of nature. Moreover, in order to be one with nature, people in these postmodern times need to turn their sights toward feminine spirituality. Female values have been distorted and even discarded by male values, and a fear of the feminine has been engendered in the unconsciousness of men. The stronger this unconscious fear toward women becomes, the more contempt for women arises and the more the tendency to control women by force emerges. Couldn't we also say that, by accepting feminine spirituality, men can be freed from their unconscious fear of women and thus find release from the need to be all-controlling that such fear creates in them?[6]

Women of today who have lost their feminine spirituality and creativity can be regarded as women who have lost their hands. So, in chapter 1 I take up a famous story—"The Handless Maiden"—from the brothers Grimm and discuss it from this perspective. As we see how the heroine recovers her lost hands, we form ideas on how to recover our spirituality. In chapter 2 I talk about what feminine creativity is. There I examine two well-known women artists, Camille Claudel and Frida Kahlo, and discuss both their personal agonies and what their creative activities meant for them. In chapter 3 I point out some remnants of feminine spirituality in today's world. I discuss the cult of the Black Virgin in Europe and that of the Senju Kannon (bodhisattva) in Japan. Although the cultural backgrounds are quite different, these phenomena nonetheless exhibit some similarities that point to the universality of feminine spirituality. In chapter 4 I discuss ways to recover feminine spirituality and creativity using clinical materials.

CHAPTER 1

The Story of the Handless Maiden

When I began working as a psychotherapist, I had an opportunity to meet a number of extraordinary women. They were exceptional in the sense that they had wonderfully unique natures. However, not a single one of them recognized her special traits. Each woman had evaluated herself according to the standards of others, which resulted in a self-dissatisfaction of sorts. Each lacked self-confidence and was unable to comprehend the worth she possessed as a person. Those who at first appeared to be self-confident were in all actuality covering up their insecurities. Unable to see themselves through their own eyes, they looked at themselves instead through the eyes of others, or they regarded themselves as they thought others (particularly males) perceived them. Their happiness and sadness were grounded in others, and they tended to bear grudges against and blame others instead of holding themselves responsible for their feelings. Listening to these women tell their stories, I began to realize that something vital was absent in their lives. What was missing was the marrow or core of their psyche. In order to stand on their own two feet without relying on other people, women need a "backbone" that sustains them. I have found this backbone to be missing in many women's lives.

This is a very serious situation. In these women's psyches there is a gaping hole or a dark void. Of course, they are not conscious of it. Yet, when I think of the increase in the number of women who are suffering from eating disorders as well as other problems such as addictions to drugs, sex, and shopping in recent years, my impression is that they are behaving as if they are trying to fill up this emptiness. Women who are consumed with their careers yet are still dissatisfied may also be trying to fill the hollow space in their soul.

Some of you may be thinking, "Nothingness is a woman's true self." It is said that an empty container is a symbol of a woman because its inner space can receive anything that comes its way. This thought is not a recent one but comes from ancient times, as does the idea that it is a man's role to fill this empty space. In ancient Greece, an empty uterus was thought to be the root of sexual dissatisfaction and the cause of hysteria. Sigmund Freud compares the female sexual organs to a box. Erik Erikson places importance on the inner space of females.[1] However, we might consider the notion that women are containers who are willing to receive things that are put into them as a thought that has arisen from the male point of view and for their own convenience. Is the true essence of women to be passive receivers? What is the fundamental nature of an object that can be recognized as an entity only after it has been filled with something from outside? This idea springs from consideration of the biological differences between males and females. However, human beings are both active and passive creatures, and without utilizing both active and passive traits, humans cannot survive. Thus the idea that either gender is wholly active or wholly passive is somewhat unnatural.

I have found feminine spirituality to be missing in women in today's world. Within analytical psychology, many Jungian analysts are also considering this same idea—that women need to return to their true selves—and they are giving various names to this idea. For example, Marion Woodman takes Sophia as an image of the feminine consciousness that women of today should recapture. Some women try to retrieve the true essence of femininity, which they have lost, by imagining the ancient goddesses. In fact, we can learn from ancient goddesses not only about loving and being loved by the male, but also about the strength of their aggressive acts and their courage in dealing with death. These goddesses are active—not passive. Helmut Barz's notion of "matriarchal animus" is his way of saying that women are capable of being active. James Hillman's "anima consciousness" describes the feminine element that present-day women need.[2] However, when I discuss feminine spirituality, I am not thinking only about feminine consciousness. Rather, I also have in mind something that is perhaps more nebulous, a concept that is not strictly divided between the conscious and unconscious levels.

Jung's notion of anima includes some aspects of feminine spirituality. Although Jung himself did not recognize anima in the feminine psyche, we can consider feminine spirituality as such because it is something like a feminine soul. Of course, we must remember that Jung's anima is an idea that he developed for male psychology; it does not directly correspond to feminine spirituality. Instead, feminine spirituality might include the aspects of both anima and animus. Even though it includes the latter, I prefer not to regard the animus as a masculine aspect but rather a part of the feminine nature.

Feminine Creativity

I am always impressed by the abundant creative potential—although it is almost entirely hidden—of the women that I meet in my psychotherapeutic practice. It seems as if, before even trying something new, they give up. By saying, "I couldn't possibly do that," they seem to blow out their own fire, or they have used this fire in a destructive way to offend the people around them as well as to hurt themselves. I have often thought that if these women would channel their energy into creative pursuits, they would not be so tormented. How should we consider eating disorders, borderline personality disorders, and dissociative disorders, all of which are problems that seem to plague mainly women? I think that if women want to help themselves recover from these problems, they must recognize their creative nature. When they awaken it, they will at the same time be able to recover their feminine spirituality.

The Victorian age (during the latter part of the nineteenth century) saw a high incidence of hysteria, a phenomenon that might well have been a direct result of the tight controls placed on women at that time. Breuer's famous patient, Anna O, who is now known to have been Bertha Pappenheim, was able to recover from hysteria via her social-welfare activities.[3] This is an excellent example of the relationship between feminine creativity and mental disorders. In comparison with that era, modern times grant much more freedom to women, and the roads to higher education are not closed to women as they once were. Women now have many opportunities to allow their natural gifts to blossom and grow. However, they still see and evaluate themselves through men's eyes, and no matter how much they accomplish, it appears that many of them are dissatisfied with themselves. Perhaps one reason for this is that, after they remove the masculine aspects that they have incorporated into their lives, there is nothing left to replace them. In other words, without the masculine framework, they find no core of femininity that sustains them. I feel that the recovery of the feminine soul is a vital issue for today's women.

When considering feminine creativity, perhaps the first thing that comes to mind is the biological ability of women to carry and give birth to children. For example, don't you ever wonder why, historically, very few women artists stand out or have made a name for themselves? One common answer for this is, "In order to show proof that a man lived, he needs to leave a piece of work for the following generations to enjoy. However, for a woman to leave proof that she lived, she needs only to produce a child for the next generation." At some point, women began to accept this concept without question, thus making it their self-destiny and fulfillment to give birth to and raise children. Indeed, this is a very special and important role that women fulfill. However, if the only road for women to take is that of childbirth and child rearing, then the necessity of having a child is obvious. Without offspring, a woman finds it very difficult to stand on her own two feet and be independent. If an individual does not recognize herself as a woman prior to becoming a mother, then she will become quite dependent on her children and control them to such a point that they will not have lives of their own. In one sense, a woman who envisions herself only as a mother closes off her creative side. This in fact might make her envious of her children and even cause her to resent them. In the name of maternal love, children become fettered, and the various seeds of possibility that the children might have nurtured instead become suppressed or buried. This is a serious problem in present-day Japan and is quite evident in the number of children who are so stymied by maternal control that they refuse to go to school or become recluses.

I do not think there is anything strange about considering the hands as a symbol of feminine creativity. However, considering the hands as an aspect of women's spirituality—this is perhaps a little unusual. One reason for this is that the hands have an active image associated with them. However, the image that is so often connected with women is a passive one, which is quite contrary to such an active perception. Of course, hands can also be passive. There isn't one of us who doesn't remember scooping up water from a stream and drinking from a container—one formed by their own hands. Since the hands have both an active and a passive side, couldn't we also say the same for feminine spirituality? I would like to consider feminine spirituality from this dualistic concept.

The subject of this book is not something that occurred to me suddenly. The idea that the hands represent feminine spirituality came to mind while I listened to my female analysands' dreams concerning hands. I was impressed with those dreams because the hands that appeared in them were often cut, injured, or decaying. These images also appeared in the women's drawings.

A young professional woman had the following dream: "I had to hold the hand of a girl because it was going to be amputated. I tried to find an adequate position, holding her hand by my hand. Then I held it by big tweezers. In the end, in order to minimize the damage, only the index finger was amputated—rather roughly by a saw. Then someone talked about the necrosis of this finger. The girl's foster family said, 'If we knew this would happen, we would not have adopted the girl.' I think it is not the girl's fault, and I am angry at the selfishness of the foster parents." In this dream the analysand helped to cut off the girl's finger. Although she rationalized this assistance by noting that the finger was already damaged by necrosis, the dream image is striking. Here a woman lent her own hand to help amputate a girl's finger. When hearing this woman's dream, I began to think of a famous fairytale by the Grimm brothers, "The Handless Maiden."

Figure 1.1. Hands drawn by a young woman. Anonymous.

I recently learned that not just a few girls have repeatedly cut their hands and arms in a self-destructive behavior called "wrist cutting." Why do they maim themselves this way? Some people conjecture that they are doing it not because they want to kill themselves, but because they want to *affirm* themselves. In other words, they cannot feel themselves living unless they cut and see themselves bleed. However, this repeated wrist cutting can also be viewed as a behavior that makes them conscious of their hands. Perhaps in today's society we have come to see the hands as just another tool. However, these young girls may unconsciously be trying to remember or recall a deeper meaning of their hands.

"The Handless Maiden" is one of the most impressive of the Grimms' fairytales, and it is remarkable that this same basic story is found in folk stories around the world, including Japan. In some versions of the tale, only the hands are cut off, whereas in other renditions the arms are cut off. Many different psychological interpretations of this story have been put forth. However, I would like to consider this story from the point of view of feminine spirituality, in particular when considering the creative and spiritual aspects of the hands. The heroine's loss of her hands can also be seen as the loss of her feminine spirituality.

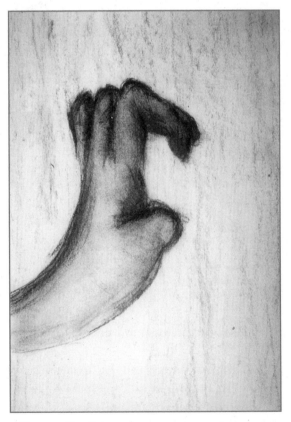

Figure 1.2. Hands drawn by a young woman. Anonymous.

Figure 1.3. A young woman's drawings. Anonymous.

The Beginning of "The Handless Maiden"

Grimms' "Handless Maiden" begins as follows:

A miller has fallen into poverty and one day meets an old man in the forest. The old man says, "I will make you rich if you promise to give me what is standing behind your mill." The miller assumes the old man means the apple tree, so he gives his promise to the old man. The old man then says, "I will return in three years and take what you have promised to me," and then vanishes. When the miller returns home, his wife asks about his newfound wealth. She then tells him that the old man must have been talking not about their apple tree but about their daughter, and that the old man must have been the devil. The miller's daughter is a beautiful, pious girl, and she spends the next three years in devout worship. At last the day arrives when the devil comes to claim the girl. That day, she washes and then

Figure 1.4. A young woman's drawings. Anonymous.

The Story of the Handless Maiden   (19)

draws a circle around herself with chalk. The devil appears, but he cannot come near her. Angered, he snatches the water away from her so she cannot wash herself again. When he returns the next day, the girl has wept on her hands, and they are now quite clean. She uses the tears in her palms to clean herself, and the devil still cannot come near. Furious, he orders her father to cut off her hands. The miller is shocked and tries to refuse. However, the devil threatens him by saying that, if he does not sever his daughter's hands, his own life will be endangered. So the miller goes to the daughter and begs her to allow him to cut off her hands. She replies, "Dear father, do with me what you will, for I am your child." Then she allows her father to cut off both of her hands. However, when the devil returns, she has wept so much on the stumps where her hands once were that they are still clean. Thus he gives up his intention to seize her for himself. The girl's father wants to continue to provide for her, but she refuses. She has her arms bound behind her back and then sets out on a journey.

Unimaginably cruel things often happen in fairytales. This story, in which a father cuts off his daughter's hands, is a powerful example. The victimized daughter does not resist her father, who is blinded by his own desires. She accepts her fate and obediently extends her hands to him. Thinking about the story, we might feel that, in modern society, we may have forgotten an important truth in our pursuit of material wealth. In the story, the daughter is portrayed as a very religious person. She has a pious spirit, which contrasts with material things. To me it seems important that a woman depicts this virtuous spirit. Why does the miller cut off his daughter's hands even though the devil cannot touch her? The miller initially has no thought of giving his daughter to the devil; he believes he is giving up only an apple tree. The daughter, however, resembles the tree, which blooms and bears fruit. The tree not only expresses the creation of life but also reminds us of the apple tree from which Eve ate the fruit of wisdom after the snake induced her to do so.

Why does the devil fear the girl's hands? He must know their value even though the miller does not. According to the story, the daughter sheds her tears into her hands, and the tears cleanse them. Thus unable to touch her, the devil becomes enraged and orders the miller to sever his daughter's hands.

The devil's fear of the girl's hands is explained more clearly by a similar story from the Balearic Islands. According to this version, a count who loses a wager becomes penniless and promises a strange man—the devil, in fact—to one day exchange his child for the ability to win every bet he places in the future. When the count's daughter becomes nine, the count takes her to the devil in accordance with his promise. Along the way, the daughter, who is very religious, prays at the shrine of the Virgin Mary. The statue of Mary opens her mouth, promises not to forsake the girl, and gives her a rosary. The daughter continues praying, shedding tears all the while. The devil becomes furious, snatches the rosary from the girl's hand, and throws it far away. However, the girl keeps on saying the rosary by counting with her fingers. The devil is so upset that he cuts her hands off. However, even after he lops off her hands, the girl continues to pray by saying the "Hail Marys" aloud, and her tears fall like the beads of a rosary. In the end, the devil abandons his desire to possess her.

This typical scenario of a father and his obedient daughter suggests that most women in modern society accept masculine values without questioning them. A negative image of masculinity is depicted as a devil who removes a female's hands with her own acquiescence. Moreover, the girl who has lost her hands continues to swallow what the male personality says and tries to force herself into the frame imposed on her by the male.

In the rendition often told in Japan, it is the father who cuts off his daughter's hands. However, because Japan does not have a Christian background, it is not the devil that entices the father to do so, but rather a stepmother. A woman in such a role also occurs in tales from Russia and France. However, Hans Dieckmann points out that this negative feminine image represents repressed femininity in a patriarchal society.[4] In the Japanese tale, the stepmother hates the daughter, but the girl is so wise that the stepmother cannot contrive to harm her. When the daughter turns fifteen, the stepmother tells her husband that she will leave him unless he throws the daughter out of the house. Afraid of losing his wife, the father says that he will take the daughter to a festival. Instead, he takes her deep into the mountains, and when the daughter becomes tired and falls asleep, he cuts her hands off and leaves her. However, in this story the girl cries out, "Oh, how terrible! Why would my father hurt me like this!" The difference here is that the heroine does not meekly accept her fate as she does in the Grimms' version.

The enemy of women's creativity is their jealousy. This is because in a patriarchal society, women always look to men and try to be liked by them. Thus women are always mutual rivals. The patriarchal society sometimes empowers the negative side of the female. Given that fact, there are not many differences between the devils and the stepmothers who make the fathers cut off their daughters' hands. Of course, what is evident in the Japanese story is the weakness of the father, who dutifully obeys his wife, which is somewhat unique to the Japanese culture. The negative aspects of the feminine may be more empowered in Japan than in other countries.

The Development of the Fairytale

The story continues:

> The daughter walks all day and stops at nightfall. She has arrived at a royal garden, and in the moonlight she sees that the trees there are covered with fruit. However, she cannot enter because the garden is surrounded by water. She is very hungry, so she begins to pray. Suddenly an angel appears before her and makes a dam in the water. After a short while, the moat dries up, and the girl is able to enter the garden. There, using only her mouth, she eats a pear. However, the king who owns the garden knows exactly how many pears he has on each tree, and when he realizes the next day that one is missing, he questions the gardener. The gardener tells him that a spirit without hands had been led to the garden by an angel and that she ate the now-missing pear with her mouth. That night the king decides to watch and takes

a priest with him. As on the night before, the maiden comes out of the thicket and begins to eat a pear. The priest comes forward and says, "Do you come from heaven or Earth? Are you a spirit or a human being?" She says that she is an abandoned human. Hearing that, the king says that he will not forsake her, and he takes her with him into his royal palace. He loves this beautiful, pious girl with all his heart, and he has silver hands made for her and then makes her his wife.

In the Grimms' story, the dauntless daughter sets out on her journey even though the miller, her father, tries to stop her. In another version collected by the brothers Grimm, the devil does not appear. Instead, the father tries to marry his daughter, but when she refuses to comply, he becomes very angry, cuts off her hands and breasts, and drives her away. The father plays the devil's role in this story.[5] When we think of female creativeness, the problem of father-daughter incest becomes a controversial issue. At any rate, to leave one's father's home is a crucial factor in developing one's creativity. Without this separation from her father, a daughter will create only what will please him, thus destroying her feminine self.

In the Grimms' story related here, the handless maiden starts walking alone, leaving her fate to heaven. Despite her impairment, God does not give up on her. An angel leads her to the royal garden, where she eats the king's pear. She likely receives wisdom from the pear (which resembles an apple), but we must recognize that the pear is different from the fruit of feminine wisdom because it is under the control of the king and, more than anything, lacks the color red. It is significant that the priest asks the handless girl, who appears to be led by an angel, "Are you a spirit or a human?" As we have discussed earlier, the hands are the one thing that makes us human. And if we think of them as an aspect of feminine spirituality, losing them would be tantamount to losing the core of one's femininity. When such a situation befalls a woman, she also loses her intuitive life and sinks into depression. It is difficult to see a positive attitude in such a woman because, even though her life has been spared, she lives in deep sorrow.

Although an angel or some other messenger from heaven does not appear in stories from the Balearic Islands or Japan, the girls in these stories survive by eating fruits, grass, or nuts from trees. In other words, nature sustains them. On the other hand, in a story from the province of Bretagne (France), a girl has a dog that brings her food. Although she remains praying in the top of a tree, her instincts work so that she may survive.

In each of the fairytales, a person of noble birth appears and marries the girl. A handless woman might be an ideal bride for a male in the sense that she has to depend on her husband completely. Jung says that a type of woman who is like an empty vessel may be the most favorable bride—from the male point of view—because the husband can impose on her any anima image he wishes. A handless woman may be such a bride because she has lost her feminine spirituality and creativity; that is to say, she has lost the core of her female soul. Again according to Jung, another reason this kind of female makes a perfect bride is that she unconsciously reflects her inner abilities to her husband instead of recognizing them as her own, and she admires the husband, who looks greater than he really is thanks to these factors.[6] In the Grimms' story, the king gives silver hands to his wife, possibly because she has eaten a pear in his garden. To put it another way, he gives her only the beautiful, substantial shape of false hands without actual blood running in them. It is important to remember that the male can never give a woman the feminine spirituality that she has lost. It is a woman's task to recover it.

When a woman feels insecure because of the loss of her feminine soul, she tries to improve her intelligence and to survive by depending on it. In the stories we have been examining, marriage to a man can be understood as the natural action of such a woman. There are many women like this in today's world. It seems that women like this gain confidence from such an attitude and try to stand on a par with men. Nevertheless, even if the situation appears satisfactory to them, their "hands" are only silver, manmade hands.

Now let's return to the story.

After a year, the king has to go to war. Because his young wife is with child, he asks his mother to come and care for her and to send him a letter when his wife gives birth. When she delivers a beautiful son, the king's mother immediately sends him a letter with the good news, but the messenger falls asleep by a brook along the way. While the courier is sleeping, the devil, who is still angry about losing the young woman, exchanges the real letter for another one that states that the young wife has given birth to a monster. When the king receives the letter, he is shocked but sends a message back saying, "Please take care of my wife until I return." However, the messenger—once again fatigued from the journey—falls asleep in the same place while on his way back to the palace. The devil once again exchanges the king's letter with a message that orders, "Kill my wife and child." The king's mother does not believe the letter and sends another letter to the king. However, the devil plays the same trick again. Finally the king's mother receives a letter ordering her to save the queen's eyes and tongue to prove to the king that she has been killed. The elderly mother pretends to have killed the queen and her baby son by killing a deer, removing its tongue and eyes, and saving them. She then tells the queen that she and her baby son have to leave the castle. And so, with the baby bound to her back, the young queen weeps piteously as she departs from the castle.

As we have just seen, the heroine finds temporary peace by marrying a man, but it is disrupted when her husband has to leave her and go out into the world. The husband asks his mother to take good care of his pregnant wife. Soon the heroine gives birth to a very beautiful child. The mother tries to send the good news to her son, but the incident of the exchanged letters occurs.

At this point, the devil, who had disappeared in the first part of the story, reappears and plays foul with the young woman's happiness. He, who had desired the young girl and then ordered the miller to sever his daughter's hands, stands in the heroine's way again. The devil has been looking and waiting for a chance to wreak vengeance on the pious daughter. In the Japanese rendition of the story, the stepmother plays the role of the devil, and a messenger happens to stop by the stepmother's house to rest. The stepmother, who hears from the messenger that her stepdaughter has given birth to a child, is consumed with hatred and exchanges the letter for one that she writes while the messenger lies in an alcohol-induced sleep. In all of these stories, the news that the heroine has given birth to a beautiful baby is always changed to say that the newborn baby is ugly or a dreadful monster, and that terrible information is what is delivered to the husband.

This scene prompts us to consider what feminine creativity is for females. In a relationship with a man, the heroine becomes pregnant and gives birth to a child with the help of the king's mother, who has a positive maternal image. It seems ideal for the female in order to achieve a level of creativity. Yet, why does the continual exchange of letters develop the story? To answer this, we must recognize that letters convey only written words; moreover, the words are not exchanged directly between the wife and the husband but between the mother and her son. We should also not forget that the new mother has no hands. Therefore she cannot write her message herself. Even though she has borne the child, the messages about the child are sent back and forth without her even knowing. The handless maiden, who has had her feminine spirituality taken away from her, can achieve good results to some extent by intensifying male intelligence. However, this does not mean that she is able to show her creative abilities based on her feminine core. Some may praise her for the talents, but others may deprecate her. In either case, she is swayed by them. A handless maiden is unable to evaluate the results herself. Moreover, she has no words of her own by which to understand it.

Because she does not have her own words, the heroine has to leave the palace under the maternal protection of her mother-in-law, and she sets out on a journey once again. The second journey is the same as the first one with respect to her helplessness. However, this time our maiden is not alone but carries her very dependent infant on her back.

What is expressed in the development of this story is that feminine creativity is not just the ability to give birth to children. If becoming a mother is the only way a woman can live her life, then she will eventually stop living it for herself and will instead try to live through her children.

The End of the Story

Let's see what happens next in the story:

> The young queen goes into the forest and prays to God. An angel then appears and takes her and her baby to a small house. A young virgin, as white as snow, comes out of the house to meet the queen and the child, and she sees to their every need. Seven years pass. Eventually, and by the grace of God, the hands of the trusting and pious young queen grow back.
>
> Soon after the young queen has left the castle, the king returns from the war, but he is quite surprised to find that his wife and baby are not there waiting for him, so he asks his mother where they are. The elderly woman replies, "You are such a terrible person. I did exactly as you ordered me to do," and she shows him the two letters that the devil had sent her. The mother is shocked when she sees the anguished expression on the king's face; she realizes that the letters are not from him. She then tells him that his wife and baby are still alive. The king decides to go looking for his wife and offspring and says, "I will not eat or drink until I find my wife and child."
>
> The king spends seven years looking here and there for his wife and child. Finally he comes upon a forest, and there he finds a small house. A white angel comes out of the house and invites the king inside. Deciding to rest there, he lies down and covers his face with a handkerchief. The angel calls the queen and her son, named Sorrowful, and they look upon the king where he is resting. The handkerchief falls off of the king's face, and the queen tells her son to pick it up. "Sorrowful, pick up your father's handkerchief and cover his face again." Upon hearing these words, the king wakes up and says to the young queen, "Who are you?" "I am your wife, and this is your child, Sorrowful," she answers. The king sees the young woman's hands and cannot believe what she has said. "Thanks to the grace of God, my hands have grown back." When the angel brings the silver hands that the king had made for the queen, he finally believes

that he has found his long-lost wife and child and is overcome with joy. The three of them return to the home of the king's elderly mother, and the king and his wife are married once again. They live happily ever after.

In this part of the story, the young maiden has the child bound to her back and once again sets out on a journey of unknown destination. However, because of her strong religious faith, an angel appears and takes her to a small house in the forest. We might wonder about the identity of the "virgin as white as snow" who comes out of the house to greet the maiden. According to the story, she is an angel sent from God to help the young queen and her baby. However, since the angel assumes a female form, we might say that she is the queen's anima— her soul. Our heroine and her baby stay at this house for seven years and receive this angel's help. During this time, the queen's hands grow back. The queen allows the angel to take care of her body during this period, and we can take this as a sign that the heroine is allowing her feminine spirituality to emerge. If we make this assumption, it would be quite natural for her hands to grow back.

In some versions of this story, including the Japanese one, when the heroine bends down to get a drink of water, her child nearly falls—or in fact does fall—into the water. In trying to save the child, the distraught heroine tries to use her hands, completely forgetting that she has lost them. But in her frantic attempt, her hands grow back. In the story from Bretagne, the heroine has twin babies, and in order to save them one by one, her right hand and then her left hand grow back. In this version of the tale, a little bird encourages the heroine by singing, "Put your arm stumps into the spring water, and do not fear for your children."

I think these stories give us a clue as to how to recover our lost feminine spirituality. For example, even if we cannot see that spirituality today, we should have belief in the hands that once were there and not be afraid to use them. When we try to save a drowning child, such an act is not prompted simply by maternal love. Mothers have a responsibility to care for the life they have brought into this world. Today we have so far been unable to place a value on feminine spirituality, or perhaps we do not know exactly what it is. However, women should be able to recall or remember the hands they have lost. To believe and trust in this means that women will be able to recapture themselves, and with this, then, their creative selves will also come forth and claim the prominence they deserve.

The time that our heroine spends in the forest signifies a very important period of necessary reflection for women. It is here that women must return to be in harmony with nature. In order for the creative side of a woman to work, she must be protected from chores and noise and isolate herself in a place where she can hear her own inner voice. Then she must once again polish her senses, which have become dulled, so that she can fully understand the little bird's song. If she does that, then she will be able to successfully raise her child.

You may be wondering why the child's name in this story is "Sorrowful." I think this is an expression of one attribute of things women create. If a woman lives in harmony with the natural world as well as with her inner nature, she will be able to recognize her true creative self. By accepting nature, whether we willingly realize it or not, we are able to live—because of the special gifts of other living things. That is a very sad thing in one sense, but we must swallow this sadness and sublimate it so that the special gift of our lives may be sustained. Our life is transient and limited, and because of that, it is sorrowful—but still beautiful. In the Japanese aesthetic sense, this is called "monono-aware," or pathos.

At some point we must take our children out into the world. In order to do that successfully, women must recover first their true selves and once again come into contact with the masculine in the world. In the story of the handless maiden, the husband who returns from war abstains from eating and drinking for seven years as he goes about searching for his wife and child. His attitude and actions are quite a contrast to those of the father, who sells his daughter to the devil in return for wealth. In order for the husband and wife to meet again, the time that they spend apart is quite important. For the woman, it is a chance to recover her creative spirit by leaving the framework of the masculine and experiencing the freedom to sustain herself. Finally, the husband finds his wife and child in the house in the middle of the forest. Even though the husband sees his wife, he cannot at first believe it is she—because her hands have grown back. Only when the angel shows the husband the wife's silver hands can he believe that he has truly found his long-lost spouse. Here we see the masculine trait of not believing something that cannot be seen. The second wedding ceremony indicates that the woman respects her true self. In other words, after the recovery of her feminine spirituality, she is able to marry her husband in the true meaning of marriage. In the Japanese story, the reunited couple is so happy that they shed tears of happiness, and beautiful flowers blossom wherever their tears fall. Also, when the couple and their child journey homeward, the road they take is covered with blossoming trees and flowers. That is truly a happy ending celebrating the joy of life.

Lost Hands and Feminine Spirituality

Marie-Louse von Franz interprets the Grimms' story as the psychological process of the heroine's liberating herself from her father complex and regaining her true self. The severing of her hands is a sacrifice on her part in order to evade an internal devil—the negative animus—and it thus indicates the heroine's passiveness. Dieckmann explains this story as the case of a woman who suffers from compulsive disorders, and he states that the cutting off of her hands signifies the paralysis of psychic activities as well as the regression into the oral stage of development. Clarissa Pinkola Estés beautifully interprets this story as a process of initiation into womanhood. The removal of the hands is compared with the rites of becoming a shaman, in which the initiate must sometimes undergo dismemberment as a mystical experience. Hayao Kawai, a Japanese Jungian analyst who interprets the Japanese version of this story, sees the heroine as a woman who endures suffering, and he explains a characteristic aspect of the Japanese ego, both male and female, with this image. According to him, the severing of the hands means that one cannot approach the outer world. Takao Oda, also a Japanese Jungian analyst, deepens his understanding of borderline personality disorder with this story. He interprets the cutting off of the hands as the amputation of aggression and an injury that one incurs when one has no means of self-defense.[7] Each of these interpretations is understandable, but for me, the heroine's loss of her hands represents women's deprivation of feminine spirituality and creativity.

One reason for my analysis has to do with the religious aspect of this story, which is one point that the Grimms' story has in common with the other versions, including the Japanese rendition. In these stories, the heroine prays to a deity. In the Grimms' story, both the devil and an angel appear, which is evidence of Christianity's strong influence. However, as the tale develops, the role that nature plays—or the role of the white virgin or angel in the healing and restoration of the hands—is for me evidence of the existence of a tie between nature and feminine power. In the version from the Balearic Islands, the heroine's faith in the Virgin Mary is obvious. Von Franz states, "only a religious experience can help the woman out of her difficulty."[8] However, this religious experience is not one that occurs as a result of the problems of a small ego; rather, it is one that prompts people to put their difficulties in the hands of something greater than their ego. Isn't that voice the one we should all listen to? I believe the ability to do this comes from feminine spirituality.

This disposition is the essence of women. I have come to this conclusion because in Okinawa, an island in the southwest archipelago (Ryukyu) of Japan, a very old tradition remains. People there believe that women have an innate spiritual quality that men lack, and the women thus assume the important roles in religious rituals and festivals, whereas men are engaged in secular matters.[9] Most likely this was also true in the rest of Japan in ancient times because there are remains of records of a Queen Himiko, who ruled the country in the third century. It is said that she had shamanlike powers and that her younger brother was head of the government. In those days Okinawa was not a part of Japan but instead was an independent kingdom. Buddhism was introduced to Okinawa very late in the seventeenth century, and this male-female tradition endured there—but not in Japan—because Buddhism's influence was much less invasive than in Japan. Unfortunately, the framework of this Okinawan tradition has in recent years undergone many changes. Even so, in some ways it still remains. One remarkable aspect of that culture is the fact that the sister-brother bond is quite strong, and a man's sister is considered to be his guardian spirit.

I do not know whether this phenomenon has occurred only in the Japanese culture. However, it is interesting to note that in the version of the "Handless Maiden" from the province of Bretagne, the sister-brother relationship is the main theme. In this account, the brother and his sister are very close; however, the brother's wife comes between the siblings, and her interference results in tragedy. Inflamed by jealousy, the brother's wife kills their cows and horses. She then blames the sister for this sinful act. She wants her husband to throw his sister out, but he does not. Finally his wife kills the couple's own son and charges the sister with the crime. This time the brother becomes very angry, cuts off his sister's arms, and leaves her in the forest. He does so because he believes his wife's words rather than his sister's.

In Bretagne, a strong remnant of the Celtic culture still remains. In Celtic legend, Priestess Morgan le Fey and King Arthur are sister and brother. As in ancient Japan, where the sister was in charge of religious ceremonies while the brother was in charge of governing, a similar structure is evident. In the story from Bretagne, the brother does not believe what his sister says. When he severs his sister's arms, he is in effect disposing of feminine spirituality, and there is a parallel here for us to consider. When the brother does not believe his sister's protestations of innocence, his legs are pierced by a thorn. Perhaps this is nature's own punishment. The thorn that pierces his flesh then begins to swell, and a tree emerges from that spot and grows quite rapidly. The brother is then unable to move. The only person that can save him from his predicament is of course his sister—after she regains her hands.

As this story demonstrates, the recovery of feminine spirituality, which is necessary for women to regain their dignity, is important not only for women but also for men. If we think of this in terms of Okinawan thought, in a patriarchal society men placed women under their control by cutting off the women's hands; however, in doing so, men lost their own guardian spirits.

In today's society women have lost their spiritual and creative hands, probably without knowing it. Women may not even remember the pain they felt when their hands were amputated. Or perhaps they have willingly allowed their hands to be cut off. In order to recover these lost members, women need to restore their harmonic relationship with nature, and they also need to be alone so that they can look deep within themselves. Perhaps this is the important lesson we derive from this story.

CHAPTER 2

Hands as a Symbol of Feminine Creativity

I will never forget the shock I felt when I saw *The Hand,* Camille Claudel's sculpture in a 1996 exhibition of her works in Tokyo. It was a small black object that was lit up by a spotlight in a glass showcase. It looked as if it were going to move. Moreover, it looked like a big spider. The work itself was very small, but it appealed to me enormously.

To open our discussion of feminine creativity, let's consider a statement by a modern Japanese artist. Tadanori Yokoo says, "When I do art, I have to be female. I must consider myself to be a shamaness. I think women have a receiving ability, whereas men have a transmitting ability which is connected to men's role in society. Moreover, men have a playing talent. It is an important balance of the two."[1] It is often said that artists are androgynous. Still, it is interesting that Yokoo refers to himself as a shamaness. Perhaps he does so because he recognizes that women have a creative spiritual quality that men lack. But I wonder whether women make the best use of this quality. Aren't they satisfied with using this ability only in their relationships with men?

What does feminine creativity look like? I would like to consider some examples of female artists: first, Camille Claudel, the artist who sculpted *The Hand,* and then Frida Kahlo. Claudel is a French sculptor, and Kahlo is a Mexican painter. These two artists, though from different cultures, have several things in common. First, both were

Figure 2.1. Camille Claudel: The Hand, 1885. Bronze, 4×10×4.5 cm. Private collection. © ADAGP, Paris, 2005. Photo by Gakuji Tanaka.

their father's favorite daughter. Of course, a father's encouragement often becomes the impetus that encourages a daughter to give free rein to her creativity. When this type of relationship exists, it is often the case that the relationship between the daughter and the mother is poor. This is a great disadvantage for such a woman.

The second similarity between these two artists is that both of them met a famous male artist who was much older, like their fathers. Because of these encounters, both women were able to develop their creativity. In the case of Camille, the man was Auguste Rodin. For Frida, it was Diego Rivera. Although they were probably both destined to meet these men, they were also made miserable by them. Another characteristic these two women share is the fact that neither one could bear children, which was a source of great sorrow for both of them. Finally, both lived lives of tragedy and pain.

When examining the history of art, you will notice that very few female artists are discussed. For example, when walking around the Louvre, you will waste your time if you search for works by female artists. Of course, there are some rare exceptions. For example, because of a study by Mary D. Garrard and a film by Agnes Merlet, an Italian Baroque artist of the seventeenth century—Artemisia Gentileschi—has been rediscovered. Because some of her works were initially considered to be those of Orazio Gentileschi, her father and a famous artist in those days, we may presume that the names of other female artists have been similarly erased. Men organized and governed the world of art; thus women had many fewer opportunities to be trained as artists. Only recently has this situation changed.

In response to the feminist movement, women have begun to reevaluate female artists who have been long forgotten. For this reason, artists such as Camille Claudel and Frida Kahlo have come to light once again. Especially when considering these two artists, many women might feel perturbed by their tragic lives. This was my first reaction, too, when I read their autobiographies. And we wonder why only women are exposed to such situations. Perhaps they are victims of a male-dominated world. However, I believe that this type of thinking—that women are victims—may be a trap that immobilizes women. If we subscribe to this line of reasoning, women will never be liberated from the thought that men are strong and women are weak. In carefully examining the works of these artists and contemplating what art meant for them, we can perhaps learn something from their works instead of seeing them simply as heroines who lived out their lives in tragedy.

Camille Claudel was a pioneer because she tried to make her way in the world as a sculptor at a time when nearly all sculptors were male. Through Anne Delbee's books and film, we gain a new understanding of Claudel's life. The relationship between Camille and Rodin, her breakdown at the end of her love affair with him, and her subsequent confinement in a mental hospital for thirty years are all aspects of her life that have come to light. Such personal misfortune makes us contemplate the difficulties women face in developing their creativity.

Camille Claudel was born in Villeneuve, a small village in the Tardenois region of France, one hundred kilometers northeast of Paris, in 1864. The year before Camille came into the world, her mother bore a baby boy who died soon after birth. Her mother became pregnant again before she had recovered from the loss of her infant son. Because she was eager to have a boy, she was quite disappointed when she was delivered of a daughter. Apparently for this reason she was unable to accept the baby girl. When Camille's mother was just four years old, she lost her own mother. Therefore, though she paid careful attention to her housekeeping duties, she seemed to have little affection for her own children. Two years after Camille's birth, a second daughter was born; finally, four years later, a son, Paul, was born. Paul later became a famous poet and dramatist. Camille's father, a tax collector, was quite concerned about his children's education. His library contained a complete set of classics, and he employed a tutor for the youngsters. Villeneuve had a rich natural environment, which provided Camille with a spiritual home of sorts. Near the Claudel home was a gigantic, craggy place called "Giants," which was both picturesque and inspiring. Paul later said that this place helped to develop their imaginations.

Camille was not only intelligent and talented but also arrogant and obstinate as is evident in her sticking to her beliefs. This attitude often surfaces in a father's favorite daughter, who may be compensating for the lack of love from her mother. Camille's mother gave her the cold shoulder more and more as she began to dote on her younger daughter, whom she named after her own mother. As a result, the sisters became estranged, and Camille developed a close connection with her brother, Paul. Both Paul and Camille were artistically gifted, and his beautiful, talented, older sister was Paul's idol. On the other hand, he was also frightened by the control she exerted over him. Ever since her childhood, Camille loved making things out of clay, and her skills astonished the people around her. Why did she love modeling so much? Paul later wrote, "Sculpturing is a desire to touch. A newborn child moves his little hands nervously before he can see. He experiences a motherly joy when holding . . . clay in both hands. In handling a lump of clay, beautiful active work begins to jump around him when he has developed some skill. All this engenders the first desire within children, and this desire is satisfied by making an ark or a doll at first."[2]

Camille may have been fascinated by modeling in clay because of her unmet need for affection. She seemed to intuitively know what she wanted. Camille must also have had a God-given talent. It is true that she was unlucky to have been treated coldly by her mother. However, if she had not, then she might not have been attracted to clay and sculpting, and her genius might not have flowered to the extent that it did.

Camille's father was astonished by her clay works, and he asked Alfred Boucher, a sculptor, for his advice. Boucher appreciated Camille's talent and agreed to tutor her. Camille became conscious of a desire to become a sculptor herself and decided to go to Paris to study art. Camille's father allowed the family to move to Paris, though he himself remained in Villeneuve in order to keep his job there. He tried to give his children the best education he could. In Paris, when Camille was nineteen years old, she met Rodin, who was twenty-four years her senior. As her master, he soon recognized her talent and took her on as his assistant. Moreover, he was fascinated with her beauty, and he not only used her as a model but also desired an intimate relationship with her. Camille had great respect for Rodin, who produced active sculptures that had never been made before, and she gradually devoted herself to him. The relationship between the two was so strong that not only did they influence each other's style, but their works also show a kind of fusion. Camille worked as the "undercarver" for Rodin's works, so very likely some of the works were almost entirely made by her and then polished by him, though they were regarded as Rodin's works alone. This may have given rise to the paranoia that Camille developed, when she later insisted that he had stolen her works.

What Camille found unbearable was that Rodin would not divorce his wife, Rose Beuret, and marry her. This was an overwhelming humiliation for a proud father's favorite daughter, and Camille kept her relationship with Rodin a secret from her family. When it was later revealed, her mother never forgave her daughter for her immorality. Clearly Camille made great sacrifices to maintain her liaison with Rodin. As another example, she had an abortion at one point in their relationship, and that remained an unhealed trauma. In fact, it appears that Rodin and Camille did not get along well with each other after her abortion. Moreover, it was often rumored that Rodin helped

Figure 2.2. Camille Claudel: *The Abandonment*, 1905. Bronze, 43×36×19 cm.
Private collection. © ADAGP, Paris, 2005. Photo by Gakuji Tanaka.

her with her works, and this made her furious. She eventually tried to
leave Rodin by moving her studio. This change in their relationship
is represented in Rodin's works *The Farewell* and *The Convalescent*.
Camille was the model for these works, and the expression on her face
and of her hands is impressive. Camille's *Little Girl with Doves* evokes

her grief over the loss of her daughter. In this painting, the tiny hand of a dead child is quite moving.

Although Camille tried to leave Rodin and become independent of him, his name followed her about for a long time. Also, in those days it was quite difficult for a woman to survive as a sculptor, and the poverty that she experienced brought on a nervous breakdown. At about the same time, her brother, Paul, who was the only person she trusted and who, she believed, would not betray her, got married.

Camille and Paul

The relationship between Camille and Rodin has already been much explored, and in any event I am more interested in the relationship between Camille and Paul. This is because this particular relationship reminds me of a tight bond, like the ancient sister-brother relationship.

Figure 2.3. Auguste Rodin: The Farewell, 1892. Plaster, 38.3×45.2×30.6 cm.
Musée Rodin, Paris.

*Figure 2.4. Auguste Rodin: The Convalescent, 1892. Marble, 49×74.1×55.4 cm.
Musée Rodin, Paris.*

In a way, these two gifted people were psychologically incestuous. The way Paul idolized Camille and the fact that she was rather awe inspiring to him became a significant theme in his plays, in which he could not touch "a forbidden woman," no matter how much he adored or loved her. Paul must have had felt abandoned by his sister when she was intimately involved with Rodin. He seemed to find it very difficult to see a proud woman like Camille become a woman who practically begged Rodin to love her. During this time, Paul converted to Catholicism and became a member of Notre Dame. He looked to his faith for support in his dealings with his sister. For him, the most significant book in the Bible was the book of Proverbs. In a sense this shows that he longed for deep, feminine wisdom and furthermore that he recognized that this type of knowledge was inseparable from his soul. After his conversion, Paul entered the diplomatic service and left his sister for quite some time. It may have been necessary for him not to see the anima image that he projected in Camille disgraced by the humiliating position she assumed with Rodin. In fact, it is also probable that Rodin himself projected the image of his elder sister, who had died young, onto Camille.

Apparently Camille's inclination for Rodin—and her disregard for the love of her brother—repeated a tragedy that occurred following her transition from a sister-brother relationship to a husband-wife relationship (although Rodin and Camille were not married). As mentioned previously, in ancient Japan, a sister-brother relationship was highly regarded. This phenomenon is found not only in Japan but also in Egypt (as in the case of Isis and Osiris) and in Celtic culture. In Japanese mythology, feminine spirituality faded in importance when

Figure 2.5. Camille Claudel: Little Girl with Doves, 1898. Oil on canvas, 125×130 cm. Lucie Audouy Collection. © ADAGP, Paris, 2005.

Hands as a Symbol of Feminine Creativity (43)

couple relationships began to take on more respect than sister-brother relationships.[3]

Initially women had authority due to an inborn spiritual quality. Later they were controlled by men and became men's muses. The spiritual nature of a woman was mostly used to help a man with his own creativity, not for hers. Even today, most women may not even question the way in which their spiritual nature is used, and they may appear to be satisfied with the role they have. However, Camille had a strong sense of pride, and she did not forgive Rodin for the humiliation she suffered in their relationship.

Perseus and the Gorgon is a sculpture Camille made when she was at the end of her brother-sister relationship. It symbolizes the defeat of her feminine spirituality. The goddess Medusa, originally the goddess of wisdom, seems to be a symbol of feminine spirituality. Originally a very beautiful woman, Medusa competed with Athena for beauty, and it is said that Athena therefore turned Medusa's fine-looking hair into snakes. Because Athena was born from the head of her father, she is considered to be the symbol of convenient wisdom for men. With Athena's help, Perseus cut Medusa's head off. In Camille's sculpture, Medusa lies at Perseus's feet, and Perseus triumphantly hangs up her head but intentionally does not look at the face. As he was instructed to do, he tries to see her face only in a mirror. Camille posed for Medusa's face, which depicts both insanity and sorrow. One might say that Perseus's face resembles Paul's. The expression of Medusa's hand reaching out in anguish is arresting. It seems that Paul believed that this sculpture was Camille's last work. I wonder whether he felt that it contained some private message from his sister.

Perseus and the Gorgon shows the end of a great power—the feminine wisdom of Medusa. People were afraid of the power of her eyes, for her stare could change people into stone. They were also afraid of Medusa's all-seeing eyes, which could pierce even things unseen. In actuality, Camille's last work was not *Perseus* but *A Wounded Niobe*. Niobe, who had many children, boasted about her fertility to Leto, who had only two offspring, Apollo and Artemis. Leto became angry and ordered her children to avenge her, so they slew Niobe's children with arrows. In the case of Apollo and Artemis, a brother-sister

Figure 2.6. Camille Claudel: Perseus and the Gorgon, 1901. Marble, 224×87×110 cm. Assurance Générales de France. © ADAGP, Paris, 2005. Courtesy Mme. Reine-Marie Paris

relationship, killing children is quite symbolic. Niobe lost her children, and Zeus turned her into stone. In this instance, the power to turn people into stone lies in a male, not a female.

When looking at Camille's statue, you will notice that Niobe's breast has been pierced by an arrow, which seems to express the wounding of both Niobe and her daughter. This statue depicts the woman's part of her work titled *The Abandonment,* which symbolizes the love she felt for Rodin. When Camille lost her mainstay—Rodin—she was devastated. A wounded Niobe, who was turned into stone, may have predicted Camille's ultimate fate—she was confined for thirty years in a mental hospital. Her creativity never shone forth again. As a psychiatric patient, she refused to make any sculptures, as if she herself had turned to stone. For Camille, her hospitalization was a slow death.

In the period when Camille was making *Perseus,* she asked Paul to let her accompany him to China, where his employment was taking him. However, he refused. It seems that Paul was disappointed because he had had to abandon his desire to become a monk. Moreover, since the Chinese political situation was unstable at that time, he felt it unwise to take Camille along with him. On his way to the Orient, Paul met and became infatuated with a married woman on board ship. This married woman, whose violent temper was similar to Camille's, may have symbolized his sister. His passionate love for this "forbidden woman" continued for five years, after which time the woman decided to discontinue their relationship. A wounded and broken-hearted Paul, along with Camille, journeyed to the Pyrenees in 1905. That same year, Camille made a statue of "a thirty-seven-year-old Paul." Soon Paul recovered from his broken heart by writing a play titled "Partage de Midi" [Partition of Noon], which describes his ill-fated love affair. Then he married and returned to China with his bride. Camille, left alone in Paris, began to suffer. Her mental condition worsened to such a degree that she even destroyed some of her works. The one that is the most representative of those days is *Wounded Niobe.*

In 1913, Camille's family sent her to a mental hospital, as if they had been waiting for the death of her father, who was Camille's strongest supporter. Her mother was the one who truly desired to have Camille shut away, but the one who was actually able to arrange the confinement was Paul. It seems that he abandoned Camille in order to save face as a diplomat and in a sense to save his own life as well. It is possible that Paul was afraid of the seed of insanity, which he, like his sister, might have inherited. His essay "My Sister Camille," written in

Figure 2.7. Camille Claudel: Wounded Niobe, 1906. Bronze, 90×50×55 cm. Collection de la Musée de la Ville de Poitiers et la Société des Antiquitaires de l'Ouest, Ch. Vignaud. © ADAGP, Paris, 2005.

1951, indicates the guilt he felt for abandoning his sister in a mental hospital.[4]

Camille was very interested in Japan, and her interest strongly affected Paul. In Europe—especially France—in those days there was a boom in Japanese art called Japanesque. *Ukiyo-e*, or Japanese woodblock prints, were admired by many artists across Europe, and it is well known that Camille's work titled *The Wave* was inspired by Hokusai's *Mount Fuji through the Wave off Kanagawa*. Paul had wanted to assume a position as a diplomat in Japan; however, he first went there in 1921 as an ambassador.

Spirituality in Camille's Works

Clearly Camille's insanity is a tragedy. It is possible to psychologically interpret her condition in various ways. Susan Kavaler-Adler, who has examined many female artists' lives from the object-relation theory, explains their experiences by adopting Marion Woodman's notion of "demon lover."[5] She states that most female artists have experienced a poor mother-daughter relationship in the pre-Oedipal stage, and as a result the daughter has a dark void in her psyche. To compensate, they create a primitive, mythical father image to fill up this void. A problem then arises during the Oedipal stage, when they feel an incestuous affection toward the mythical father image, who is almost more than human. This "demon lover" with strong magical powers drives the women artists to obsessively create works of art.[6]

Such is the case with Camille. She projected an exaggerated father image onto the older Rodin. When their relationship went well, she devoted herself—mind and body—to him. Once the relationship went bad, he became a source of evil for her, and she thus began to develop a paranoid condition. According to Kavaler-Adler, the problem was that Camille was unable to overcome her depressive position in the sense put forth by Melanie Klein. That is, she could not look at the negative side within her and project the evil onto the outer world.[7] In Jungian words, a container to contain the archetype could not be formed in her early childhood because the primordial mother-child relationship was not a nurturing one. Thus, Camille was directly threatened by something archetypal. From my point of view, the dark void in Camille's psyche derived from the absence of feminine spirituality.

Of course, I can agree with Kavaler-Adler's explanation from a psychological point of view. However, I think it is not constructive to state that all of these difficulties are a result of trauma in the pre-

Oedipal stage of development. Whenever we talk about an unhappy mother-child relationship, we are apt to blame the mother. I feel that we err in thinking that a woman can identify her mother as the cause of this tragedy. Camille was an avid reader, and certainly she tried to fill up the void in her psyche with intellectual ideas since she did not receive feminine spirituality from her mother. However, we might also say that she derived much satisfaction from kneading clay with her hands. I think that modeling clay was a way for her to fulfill the innate longings that were never satisfied by her mother. Because she spent much time playing in the hills and woods around her village, I think she was something of a wild child whom nature brought up.

Paul believed there was a big difference between the individual works of Rodin and Camille. In particular, he notes the difference as seen in the spirituality of Camille's works. Paul says, "Rodin challenges a lump. Everything is complete and heavy. Everything finds its unity in a lump itself." He continues: "How completely different my sister's works are! They are, with a light and airy hand, a taste like always [being] badly drunk, a constant appearing of her spirituality, a complex penetration of all functions of inner light and ventilation or a [colony] of coral."[8]

In these differences between Rodin's and Camille's works, we can distinguish feminine creativity from the masculine type. Her works are spirituality given form, and she herself exists in all of her works. Of course, this means not only spirituality, but when a work is cut, her blood bleeds from it. Therefore, to follow the progression of works is to follow the progression of her life. For instance, Camille could not help making the piece called *The Age of Maturity* when she decided to leave Rodin. For her, to create was to live.

Rodin acknowledged Camille's originality by saying, "I taught her where gold is; however, any gold she finds is hers." The tragic thing is that Rodin's presence was so immense that Camille was not appreciated as she deserved to be. As Paul has said, "She devoted her all to Rodin, and then she lost her all with Rodin. A beautiful vessel was tossed about by the bitter waves and sank with all the cargo."[9]

The works made by her hands shine with a glimmer of feminine spirituality. This light is not bright, but it induces a feeling within

Camille's audience that they are also looking into a space beyond the forms. It is likely no accident that Camille was interested in Japanese culture.

Gérard Bouté has paid special attention to the shadow of death that is present in Camille's works. He refers to this shadow by mentioning Camille's older brother, who died only a few days after his birth. He states that, because of him, Camille felt that her mother could not love her. She felt inadequate to substitute for her older brother, and this appears in her works, which gives them a unique duality. This opinion supports the supposition that the abortion of the child that she conceived by Rodin became the trigger that caused her mental health to deteriorate. I believe that the death of her child meant the denial of her own existence. However, she tried to overcome her sorrow by creating works. Bouté refers to her work *The Wave* by saying, "Her sculpture makes an impossible desire as a metaphor under the double principle of feminine and masculine: full and empty, active and passive, solid and liquid, onyx and the sea."[10] It is the potential to change impossibility into possibility that I feel expresses the feminine spirituality in her works.

In the foreword of Jacques Cassar's book titled *Dossier Camille Claudel*, Jeanne Fayard points out that Paul Claudel regarded Camille as a descendent of a cursed poet. Moreover, she says, "It is rare to talk about a cursed female artist. In every era, such a woman was regarded as a witch or a hysteric, or in the best case, a mystic."[11] I also believe that Camille's feminine spirituality was not understood during her lifetime. She denied staying within the framework of a woman of the Victorian period. The graceful but deceitful manners of this era must have been unbearable for a wild woman like Camille. She tried to overcome the Victorian framework imposed on men and women, and as a result she was hurt—because she was a woman. I feel, however, that her nature cannot be fully understood if we cast her merely as a victim. Her insanity might be similar to that of Cassandra. Perhaps her refusal to touch clay while she was a patient in the asylum was the last vestige of pride of a neglected prophetess.

As mentioned earlier, when parting with Rodin, Camille made a work called *The Age of Maturity*, for which she herself posed. The work shows a young woman imploring a man not to leave her as he is being taken away by an old woman. Later, the young woman became independent statues called *The Implorer* and *God Flown Away*. In *The Implorer,* the expression of the woman's hands, which are grabbing at the air, is quite striking.

There are two similar statues—one with hands and one without hands. The former is called *The Fortune,* and the figure is blind. The latter is called *Truth Emerging from the Well,* and the figure is not blind but has no hands.

Camille's favorite work is *The Flute Player,* which is also called *The Little Siren.* In this work the woman's arms are looped, and the hands

Figure 2.8. Camille Claudel: The Wave, 1897. Bronze, 62×56×50 cm. Private collection. © ADAGP, Paris, 2005. Photo by Gakuji Tanaka.

Figure 2.9. Camille Claudel: The Implorer, 1899. Bronze, 28×25×16 cm. Private collection. © ADAGP, Paris, 2005. Photo by Gakuji Tanaka.

look free and easy and are placed one upon the other. The flowing music from these hands may be the feminine spirituality she wanted to express.

Camille's *The Hand* surely appeals to those who gaze upon it even today. There is feminine creativity and spirituality in that work that we have forgotten but need to recall.

The Hands of Frida Kahlo

Sometimes an expression of hands has significant meaning in art. For example, the expression of the hands of Leonardo da Vinci is characteristic. Is it too much to say that the hand is equal in weight to the enigmatic smile of da Vinci's works? His famous portrait, *Mona Lisa,* would be quite different if he had not painted her hands. Erich Neumann states that the *Mona Lisa* is a monumental work resulting from the fact that da Vinci had a "Sophia experience" when he was fifty years old. "The feminine in this painting was expressed neither as a heavenly goddess nor an earthly mother, but in a unique way, something spiritual and human. Heavenly things and earthly things are integrated again within this portrait. And there is a combination of opposites: uncertain and certain, gentle and cruel, far and near. I wonder if it is in reality or beyond time. . . . Madonna and a witch, the mundaneness and divinity become united in her."[12] One might say

Figure 2.10. Camille Claudel: The Fortune, 1900. Bronze, 48×35×17 cm. Private collection. © ADAGP, Paris, 2005. Photo by Gakuji Tanaka.

Hands as a Symbol of Feminine Creativity (53)

*Figure 2.11. Camille Claudel: Truth Emerging from the Well, 1900.
Bronze, 30.5×32.5×13.5 cm. Private collection. © ADAGP, Paris, 2005.
Photo by Gakuji Tanaka.*

that feminine spirituality is embodied in this work. Thus the expression of hands in it may be indispensable.

Frida Kahlo is quite well known because of her "injured" self-portrait, which certainly shocks viewers. Frida's life itself was both a mentally and a physically injured one. She underwent many surgical operations and endured much physical pain. As in the case of Camille Claudel, Frida never had a feeling of basic well-being from her mother, and this lack of security may have been the source of her hardships. However, I prefer to focus on the fact that she sustained herself by painting pictures. The paintings themselves contain very private material, and her attitude toward them makes me think of feminine spirituality and creativity.

*Figure 2.12. Camille Claudel: The Flute Player (The Little Siren), 1904.
Bronze, 53×27×24 cm. Private collection. © ADAGP, Paris, 2005.
Photo by Gakuji Tanaka.*

Frida Kahlo was born in Mexico in 1907 as the third daughter of
a German-Jewish father and a mother who descended from a Span-
ish conqueror and a Native American. Her mother became pregnant
again soon after she gave birth to Frida, and so Frida was raised by
a Native American nurse and later by her elder sisters. There was a
gulf in the relationship between Frida and her mother from the very

beginning. On the other hand, Frida's father was very fond of her because he thought Frida resembled him more than the other children did. This is the same pattern found among most women artists. At the age of six, Frida had to stay at home because she suffered from infantile paralysis. She was lonely but consoled herself by playing with an imaginary friend. As her father's favorite daughter, Frida had both delicate feeling and an air of arrogance. That is also common among women artists. Her father liked to paint for pleasure, so Frida began painting to please her father. Then, as if her mission were to make her father proud, she decided to become a physician and entered a national preparatory high school at the age of fifteen.

Frida's life of injury and pain began as a result of a serious accident in 1925 in Mexico City. While she was riding on a bus, a streetcar ran into the vehicle, and she was critically injured. When Frida was convalescing at home, apparently her mother recommended that she paint in order to while away the tedious hours. Although her mother apparently did not show enough affection to her daughter, she was a good manager of the household, and she had a special easel made for Frida so that she could paint in bed. Frida's mother also had a mirror set inside the canopy of the bed, and Frida used it to paint a self-portrait. That was Frida's opportunity to start painting in earnest. If this was the starting point of her career, then her mother's intervention was important.

At the time of Frida's convalescence, she sent her self-portrait to her boyfriend in order not to lose him. The expression of her hands in the painting is impressive. This present had only a temporary effect, however, and the relationship soon ended, mainly because of Frida's fickleness. It seems that she sought relationships with men in order to fill up her psychic emptiness.

Frida approached Diego Rivera, a notable Mexican painter, and showed him her paintings. He complimented her talent and encouraged her to continue painting. Moreover, he was fascinated with her provocative attitude, and, though she was twenty years his junior, he asked her to marry him. They married in 1929. It is said that Diego was an ideal father for Frida, and at the same time this stout man was a substitute for her mother. She said, "I suffered two grave accidents

Figure 2.13. Frida Kahlo: Self-Portrait in a Velvet Dress, 1926. Oil on canvas, 79.9×59.5 cm. Private collection. © 2005 Banco de México, Diego Rivera and Frida Kahlo Museums Trust. Av. Cinco de Mayo No. 2, Col. Centro, Del. Cuauhtémoc, 06059 Mexico, D.F.

in my life. One in which a street-car knocked me down. . . . The other accident is Diego."[13] This relationship marked the beginning of a new type of pain for Frida. The main source of her sorrow was Diego's inconsistency. Young Frida wanted to be her Mexican husband's favorite, so, after she and Diego were married, she wore a traditional Tehuana dress that came from the Mexican isthmus of Tehuantepec, which is known for its matrilineal society. Even so, Diego took the lead in their marriage. Frida painted a picture that commemorates their wedding. In comparison with the big hand in her self-portrait, in this painting her hands are quite small.

Diego and Frida moved to America because he was asked to make a wall painting there, but Frida never became accustomed to life in the United States. While in Detroit, she had a miscarriage, and she used painting to help get over that crisis. Also, during her stay in America, she lost her mother. Frida barely made it home in time to be by her mother's side when she died. The pain Frida experienced is evident in the picture titled *My Birth*. In it, the baby that is emerging from between the legs of the mother is Frida, and the mother seems to have already died. The head and upper part of the mother are covered by a cloth, so the hands are not seen. The statue of the Virgin Mary on the wall has an expression of anguish—and has nails driven through its throat.

While Frida was in Mexico with her dying mother, Diego had an affair with her younger sister, Christina, and Frida was shattered to learn of their betrayal. She expressed her distress in a work titled *Just a Sting*. This work is derived from a murder case in which a man tore a woman to pieces. When caught by the police, he murmured, "I just did a sting." This incident seems to symbolize man's lack of awareness of his hurting a woman. Frida traveled to New York with a female friend, and in the end she reconciled with her sister and agreed with her husband to live apart from each other. After that, she became addicted to alcohol and had many lovers, both men and women. Men were attracted to her because of her unique charm, but Diego was a special man for Frida. He was not only her husband but also her mother—her all. As Camille Claudel did for Rodin, Frida projected her all—an archetypal image of immense proportion—onto Diego.

Figure 2.14. Frida Kahlo: Frida and Diego Rivera, 1931. Oil on canvas. 100×79 cm. Museum of Modern Art, San Francisco. © 2005 Banco de México, Diego Rivera and Frida Kahlo Museums Trust. Av. Cinco de Mayo No. 2, Col. Centro, Del. Cuauhtémoc, 06059 Mexico, D.F.

In her eyes, he was practically a god. She said, "Diego is the name of love."

Among her works in those days, one stands out. It is *Memory*, painted in 1937. In this picture Frida, in the center, has no hands. Her heart is pierced and falls bleeding to the ground.

The work titled *My Nurse and I,* made in the same year, shows a baby, Frida, with an adult face suckling at the breast of a black nurse. This black nurse may represent Frida's Native American nurse, who had wet-nursed baby Frida. However, this woman figure with an Aztec mask might also be the Earth Mother, who takes care of Frida's wounded soul with her dark hands. Since the mask has eyebrows like Frida's, she might have been looking for an earthy, caring mother in herself, although her true face was still hiding under the mask. The milk coming down from heaven appears to be a blessing from above.

Frida was a favorite of the surrealist André Breton, who invited her to Paris in 1939. Her special works and her personality attracted many artists, of whom Picasso was one. He presented her with earrings shaped like hands, which she liked and often wore. Breton regarded her works as surrealistic. However, Frida denied this and said, "I never painted dreams. I painted my own reality. The only thing I know is that I paint because I need to, and I paint always whatever passes through my head, without any other consideration."[14] Surely her subjects were her reality, but they may have seemed to Breton like objects or scenes in a dream. In any event, they charmed him. Frida's feelings were depersonalized, so she may have painted her reality like a dream.

When Frida returned to Mexico, she was given a petition for divorce from her husband. At that time she painted *Two Fridas.* In this picture, one of the Fridas is wearing the Tehuana dress that Diego loved while she grasps the hand of the other Frida, who is wearing European clothes. She might have been steeling herself to deal with the torment of the impending divorce. Although she painted the same bloody heart as the one that appears in *Memory,* this time the expression of her hands shows her will to sustain herself. Of course, she was not yet completely liberated from the fixation on Diego.

Frida tried to be economically independent, but the damage of the divorce was much more severe than she expected. We cannot discern Frida's hands in *The Wounded Table,* when she was not only emotionally wounded but also in total confusion.

Her physical condition worsened during those days as well. An old friend, Doctor Leo Eloesser, advised Frida to remarry Diego for health reasons. She and Diego agreed to do so, but Diego imposed

Figure 2.15. Frida Kahlo: Memory, 1937. Oil on metal, 40×28 cm. © 2005 Banco de México, Diego Rivera and Frida Kahlo Museums Trust. Av. Cinco de Mayo No. 2, Col. Centro, Del. Cuauhtémoc, 06059 Mexico, D.F.

the condition that she accept his affairs. On the other hand, Frida insisted on splitting the household expenses and refused to continue a sexual relationship with Diego. Though they married again, Frida lived alone in her parents' home in Coyoacán, and when her pictures became popular and began to sell, she and Diego lived mostly apart. Her physical condition worsened, and she underwent operations several times as a result of a condition called "polysurgery syndrome." We cannot deny that she evoked concern from her husband by these medical procedures. On the other hand, she regarded herself as an injured person. She may have become so insecure without Diego's sup-

Figure 2.16. Frida Kahlo: My Nurse and I, 1937. Oil on metal, 30.5×34.7 cm. Dolores Olmedo Collection. Ciudad de México, © 2005 Banco de México, Diego Rivera and Frida Kahlo Museums Trust. Av. Cinco de Mayo No. 2, Col. Centro, Del. Cuauhtémoc, 06059 Mexico D.F.

port that only her physical pain reassured her that she was still alive. In 1949, Frida painted a picture named *The Broken Column*, which depicts a woman obviously in agony yet managing to rise to her feet.

The Love Embrace of the Universe, the Earth (Mexico), Diego, Me, and Señor Xolotl demonstrates that Frida had attained a sort of acceptance of her life. She holds her husband as a child in her arms, and she herself is held by a Mexican Earth Mother, who in turn is held by the universe. Frida cast her husband as a child in an effort to learn to endure his selfishness. Moreover, she even formed friendships with his lovers. In this painting, she is embraced by the big hands of the

Figure 2.17. Frida Kahlo: The Two Fridas, 1939. Oil on canvas, 173.5×173 cm. Museo de Arte Moderno, Mexico City. © 2005 Banco de México, Diego Rivera and Frida Kahlo Museums Trust. Av. Cinco de Mayo No. 2, Col. Centro, Del. Cuauhtémoc, 06059 Mexico D.F.

Hands as a Symbol of Feminine Creativity (63)

Figure 2.18. Frida Kahlo: The Wounded Table, 1940. Oil on canvas, 121.5×245 cm.
Present whereabouts unknown. Photograph courtesy of Solomon Grimberg. © 2005
Banco de México, Diego Rivera and Frida Kahlo Museums Trust. Av. Cinco de
Mayo No. 2, Col. Centro, Del. Cuauhtémoc, 06059 Mexico D.F.

universe. She put herself in the position of the mother, but the baby Diego is so big and heavy that she cannot hold him all by herself.

Frida's condition worsened in 1950, and she again painted on an easel from her bed. When she had to have her leg amputated, she was thrown into despair, and it is reported that she attempted suicide. During this time she was friends with women only. Despite these hardships in her last days, she painted a juicy watermelon and called it a living-life painting—not a still-life painting—as if she had bounced back to life. She even wrote the words "Hurrah for life" in the picture. However, on the last page of her diary she drew a black angel, and in 1954, at the young age of forty-seven, she died.

Spirituality in Frida's Works

For Frida, painting was life. When applying for the right to participate in a competition sponsored by the Guggenheim Foundation, she wrote, "I have not expected to get from my work more than the satisfaction of the fact of painting itself and of saying what I could not say in any other way." She continues, "My subjects have always been my sensations, my states of mind and the profound reactions that life has been producing in me."[15] She seemed to confirm her existence when she painted. Frida could be dependent on people and show her weakness only when she was punished with consuming pain. She may have been able to drown her suffering only on canvas. Her self-portraits are

Figure 2.19. Frida Kahlo: The Love Embrace of the Universe, the Earth (Mexico), Diego, Me, and Señor Xolotl, 1949. Oil on canvas, 59.9×60.3 cm. Jorge Contreras Chacel Collection, Mexico City. © 2005 Banco de México, Diego Rivera and Frida Kahlo Museums Trust. Av. Cinco de Mayo No. 2, Col. Centro, Del. Cuauhtémoc, 06059 Mexico D.F.

Hands as a Symbol of Feminine Creativity   (65)

Figure 2.20. Frida Kahlo: Portrait of Doña Rosita Morillo, 1944. Oil on canvas, 76×60.5 cm. Dolores Olmedo Collection, Mexico City. © 2005 Banco de México, Diego Rivera and Frida Kahlo Museums Trust. Av. Cinco de Mayo No. 2, Col. Centro, Del. Cuauhtémoc, 06059 Mexico D.F.

rather masklike images. Interestingly, only a few of her self-portraits have hands, and they are likely a more honest feature than her face.

Frida's favorite work was *A Portrait of Doña Rosita Morillo Safa*, which shows the large, strong hands of an elderly woman knitting. This picture seems to represent something that Frida longed to be.

Frida was no doubt distressed by her torturous life with Diego. Yet, without him, her works would never have been created. It is not clear whether she would have continued to paint, had her relationship with him not occurred.

Frida inherited her German-Jewish father's sense of the Diaspora. As *Two Fridas* demonstrates, this part of Frida was not accepted by Diego, who admired only her Mexican blood. Thus Frida continually needed something to believe in while holding various inconsistencies within herself. Her mother's fanatical Catholicism was little support to Frida. Perhaps she would have lived longer if her inner strength had been rooted in a deeper layer in her psyche.

It is often said that Frida Kahlo's works resemble *retablos*, small painted altarpieces. In my opinion, that is so not only because her works express her anguish but also because each brushstroke represents meditation and prayer. Every single stroke urged her to delve farther into herself, and then she was ushered out again by something emanating from the depths of her heart. This feminine spirituality in her works was, for her, the only way to bridge the internal contradictions she lived. As with Camille Claudel's works, to follow Frida Kahlo's art is to follow her life history. Her works are very personal, but they are also universal, and for this reason they move us. Diego Rivera understood this most of all. He says, "Frida's art is individual-collective. Her realism is so monumental that everything has 'n' dimensions. Consequently, she paints at the same time the exterior and interior of herself and the world. . . . But for Frida, that which is tangible is the mother, the center of all, the mother-sea, tempest, nebula, woman."[16]

Pain and Feminine Creativity

In order to explore feminine creativity, I have examined Camille Claudel and Frida Kahlo. The image of a wounded woman pursued them always. However, it would be shortsighted to view their work only from the point of view of the wounded woman. Both women worked creatively because, without working, they could not exist. Their need for creative activity was their need to live. It was also a way to affirm themselves. Surely the lack of affection from their mothers was a common thread between these two women and made their hold on life uncertain. Camille's mother, at the age of four, had lost her own mother, and Frida's mother was abandoned by her parents and raised in a convent. In both cases, their mothers may have been emotionally unable to provide nurturing maternal care. Camille and Frida thus received from their mothers neither the wisdom of feminine spirituality nor the pride of being a woman. As a result, both of them wanted to be like men; that is, they could not find approbation as women, and at the same time they used their feminine charms to attract men. Thus they were inconsistent. On the one hand, they each had an inflated self-image; on the other hand, each woman was insecure about her own self-worth. In the current classification of psychological disorders, Camille and Frida might be called borderline cases. However, they worked creatively and were somehow able to maintain their balance. The result is that a feminine spirituality that was not afforded in their environment flowers in their works.

Why did these two women have such tragic lives? It is because they both wanted affection from a man and that desire was never satisfied. They repeated the father-daughter relationship with the main men in their adult lives—men who caused them unspeakable pain. I also think that, because they allowed themselves to be victimized, they were unable to break the cycle. A victim always has a counterpart—an offender. Before someone becomes a victim in a relationship, that person must depend on and have expectations of the other person. When they are betrayed, they then become a victim. Recovering feminine spirituality and pride in being a woman means that one no longer regards oneself as a victim. If tragedy was predominant in the lives of these two women artists, the reason might be that they met a man too early in their lives—before they were able to stand on their own.

I believe that, in order for a woman to make the best use of her creativity *for herself,* she needs to be completely alone. It is a terribly lonely state, and one may walk slowly in her own path, but it is essential for one to believe in oneself. It is often said that the nature of a woman is found in a relationship. It would be wise for us to doubt the validity of this assertion. Over a long period of time, women have been indoctrinated to believe this. Women tend to give all they have to their partner in a relationship. If women are to avoid selling their souls, then being alone is all the more essential. That might be sublime in some cases; in any event, we must avoid selling our souls.

The works of Camille and Frida move us. That is because we feel that feminine spirituality is at work within them. It was engendered when the artists suffered. By knowing Camille and Frida, we can feel their anguish, but at the same time, we need to remember their strength as evidenced by the fact that they persevered in their work despite their torment. The hands of both Camille and Frida talk to us. We recognize that being creative was the only way they knew to relieve their distress. This makes these two women's hardships all the more important.

What Makes Creativity Work

C. G. Jung explains human creativity with the term "transcendent function of the psyche." When we endure a conflictual situation, this psychic function is activated. We then find a totally new way to respond in a somewhat higher dimension. This is the only process by which humans change, and according to Jung, it is this function that makes the psychotherapeutic and individuation processes work. When Jung became interested in alchemy later in life, he developed this idea even further. He believed alchemy to be the symbolic expression of the individuation process. Alchemy is also said to be a water vein of feminine spirituality. The aim of alchemy is symbolized as the marriage of a king and queen, and it is important that this marriage be a sacred one between a brother and sister. However, such a sacred union is highly significant because in reality it represents both an inviolable taboo and a strong spiritual bond between brother and sister. It goes without saying that a brother-sister relationship implies that their base is the same because they were born of the same parents, although they are different in sex. I think that there is considerable meaning here; that is, they are different but the same; they are opposite but equal. I think that feminine spirituality can be symbolized by the brother-sister (sister-brother) relationship, which is similar to the connection between our left hand and our right hand.

As in the cases of Camille and Frida, the way they began to develop their creativity was to become their father's favorite daughter. But in a father-daughter relationship, a woman must look down on herself in order to develop creativity. That is because the father is always in a higher position, and the daughter can never stand on the same—equal—ground. In such a relationship, all a woman can do is either think poorly of her feminine self or play the part of a woman who has become a man's favorite. She compels herself to fit into a framework prepared by a man, and she generously allows a part of her body to be cut off—the part that sticks out of the frame.

Robert Stein refers to the importance of the sister-brother relationship and expresses it by the word "Eros" in his book *Incest and Human Love*. "When 'Eros' is conceived as feminine, the principle of openness, receptivity, and responsiveness is stressed. As a masculine Deity, it becomes a much more active, outgoing, penetrating, and, therefore, phallic principle. Eros is at once the great opener and the great receiver—so that its true nature is hermaphroditic." He next says, "Still, it reveals itself most clearly in its active, outflowing manifestations, which explains its predominantly masculine representations."[17] It seems as though Stein is overemphasizing the sexual aspect, perhaps because his is a man's point of view. I prefer to use the words "feminine spirituality" instead of "Eros" because I believe the spiritual aspects are more important for women, although women have sexual aspects, too.

Moreover, Stein says, "Above all Eros seems to function as a mediator between the Divine and human." He states that there is a religious meaning and difference between love and Eros: "Eros desires a creative development of a particular relationship more than it desires union. Love is the basic ingredient. But Eros is the transforming vessel."[18] This idea overlaps what I would like to say about feminine spirituality.

Although Jung discusses syzygy, which refers to a pair of the interacting principles of yin and yang by gnosis, he considers anima and animus to be something peculiar to each gender. However, anima and

Figure 2.21. Auguste Rodin: The Cathedral, 1908. Stone, 64×29.5×31.8 cm. Musée Rodin, Paris.

animus cannot exist if one or the other is lacking. Therefore, most Jungians today, from Hillman on, think that both anima and animus exist in everyone. In my view, the original connection must be a sister-brother relationship.

In a mother-son relationship, as well as one between father and daughter, a man and a woman are not equal. When two people in a relationship are unequal, the connection becomes one of ruler and submitter or of offender and victim. If it is almost inevitable that we bring the images of mother-son and father-daughter into a man-woman relationship, it is because we are seized by an inflated archetype of the mother and father. That means we put ourselves in the position of a child who is always demanding more affection. I also believe it is questionable that a woman tries to absorb the image of a goddess in order to remember the feminine authority within her. Instead of claiming her power, I contend it is more important to acquire a sense of integrity.[19] We cannot find it on the outside; rather, we need to dig for it in the depths of our psyche.

Edmund Leach poses the question "Why does Moses have a sister?" and analyzes the structure of the Bible. Then he points out that Moses' sister, the "prophetess Miriam," existed in the Old Testament, but she transformed into Mary, the mother of Christ, in the New Testament.[20] The sister changed into a mother, at which time her raison d'être was to give birth to her son; thus the nature of the prophetess disappeared from the Virgin Mary. I think that women need to retrieve the position of prophetess-sister in their psyche in order to recover their lost hands.

CHAPTER 3

Hands as the Symbol
of Feminine Spirituality

Feminine spirituality remains in the Japanese culture and character, although, amid the bustle of modern society, many Japanese people are barely aware of it. Of those young people who are conscious of cultural feminine traits, many of them simply reject them. It may seem strange to people from other countries to hear that most Japanese people go to Shinto shrines on New Year's Day to pray for happiness even though they are not really religious. Buddhism is a popular family religion; however, most Japanese people first learn that their family is Buddhist when a relative dies and the family must make arrangements for a funeral. Few Japanese people pray for their ancestors every day or teach their children Buddhist doctrines. The Japanese people have a relaxed attitude toward religion. However, before Buddhism was introduced to Japan, the ancient Japanese people had a strong sense of communion and unity with nature. In fact, the origin of Shintoism—the indigenous religion of Japan—is nature worship, and the aesthetic sense of the Japanese people reflects this background.

Daisetz Suzuki, a Buddhist scholar, relates in *Japanese Spirituality* that this aesthetic sense started to blossom in the thirteenth century during the Kamakura period. At that time, Shinran Shonin (1173–1262), a monk, began to proselytize Jodo Shinshu, a new Japanese Buddhist sect. Suzuki might say that, before that time, the psyche (*kokoro* in Japanese) of the people was still very simple and Shintoism was fairly primitive. He points out that Shinran's Buddhism was significant because an integral part of it was Japanese spirituality. That is, Buddhism, which was imported into Japan, influenced the indigenous Japanese spirituality, which then became more important in people's lives. However, I believe that Japanese spirituality had begun to flourish before Shinran's time and was around even in the indigenous religion: ancient or pre-Shinto.

Suzuki also states that the Heian period (from the eighth to the thirteenth century, prior to the Kamakura period), a time when many women writers appeared at court, was quite feminine. He says, "The feeling and emotion of the Heian women were still on the periphery of Japanese spirituality."[1] I maintain, however, that the feminine quality itself is a special aspect of Japanese spirituality. Suzuki says that Japanese spirituality was established in the Kamakura period, when samurai—swordsmen—started to appear in response to Jodo (Pure Land Buddhism) and Zen Buddhism. Perhaps the reason for Suzuki's point of view is that he himself is a male.

In any event, Suzuki's idea of Japanese spirituality gives us a basis for reflecting on feminine spirituality. He first defines spirituality as a component of the inner part of the psyche and then describes it as something beyond two opposites. He says, "Spirituality is the operation latent within the depths of *seishin* [psyche]; when it awakens, the duality within the *seishin* dissolves. *Seishin* in this true form can sense, think, will, and act." He regards this spiritual experience as the religious consciousness. Here he expresses a type of wisdom that goes beyond logic and discretion. In addition, he considers spirituality to be a function that cannot be explained by the various roles of the human psyche: the senses, the emotions, the will, and the intellect.[2] His idea is very similar to Jung's idea of the transcendent function, which surpasses Jung's concept of the four psychic functions: sensation, feeling, intuition, and thinking. It is interesting that, instead of Jung's intuition, Suzuki includes the will as one of the four functions of the psyche. For Daisetz Suzuki, intuition (insight) is an attribute of spirituality instead.

Although spirituality itself is universal, Suzuki explains that every cultural group is different with respect to the way in which spiritual phenomena emerge. In speculating about Japanese spirituality, he maintains that its close connection with nature is its most characteristic trait: "Spirituality may appear to be a faint and shadowy concept, but there is nothing more deeply rooted in the earth, for spirituality is life itself."[3] Life comes from and returns to the Earth. In this way, each of us connects with the Earth, and each of us has a unique, irreplaceable existence; therefore, each one of us feels absolute aloneness. Spirituality results when one becomes aware of one's existence by connecting with and assimilating to the Self that surpasses the individual self (Suzuki calls it "supra-individual individual") in the depth of the psyche or the unconscious. In other words, each person is universal because of our ultimate individuality. (This is similar to the relationship between Jung's individuation and the Self.) Only through this spirituality can we obtain insight into the circularity of life, which gives us a notion of eternity. The individual spirit may be a mirror that reflects the universal spirit.

Suzuki also points out the importance of one's inner willingness to give oneself up to something larger. Although this at first sounds like total surrender, we need to be active at the same time. He compares the idea with the hatching of an egg, where a simultaneous pecking from both the inside and outside is needed. He says, "Though one side may be passive and the other active, if there is no activity as well there will be no possibility for any sort of response between the two."[4] This is also an important aspect of Japanese spirituality. Only with such insight can we completely accept other people as they are, although they may be very different from us.

Suzuki's Japanese spirituality may be considered as feminine spirituality. There are implications of things we may have had in ancient times and now need to recall. These are our relationship with life, which is not typically Japanese but instead reflects the universal human nature; our response to the universe, which is concrete and universal; the ability to accept situations as they are but not to be controlled by them; and the ability to make the most of ourselves. Although these are essential for both men and women, men may need some philosophical mainstay to perceive these things, as Suzuki considers them in relation to Buddhist doctrine. On the other hand, I think women may have had this kind of intrinsic sense of nature.

However, modern women may have lost this innate knowledge along the way. How can we retrieve it? Suzuki hints at the answer to this question. He says, "The working of spirituality begins from deep contemplation of the world's phenomena, progressing finally to a desire to grasp the eternally constant something that is beyond the world of cause and effect."[5] Needless to say, such contemplation is not easy to do. According to Suzuki, one can see the light only after an experience in which one is totally denied one's existence. He also says that one should not wait around aimlessly. Rather, one should be proactive in order to find and comprehend the meaning one seeks. Maybe we should reflect on ourselves as totally isolated beings, seeking for our Selves that which mirrors the universe and connects to the mystery of life. At the same time, we should cherish the present and live our lives to the fullest. Only after taking both of these steps—and if we resign ourselves to the absolute existence of all things—will we be able to draw wisdom from life and find that our prayers are answered.

Hands for Praying

In Japanese, the phrase "to join one's hands together" means "to pray." In many other countries also, people put their hands together when they pray. Maybe we are able to concentrate better by doing this. However, we do not put our hands together when we think. Joining our hands helps to bring together the input from the different parts of our brain. Usually we place our hands together in front of our chest—not near our head but near our heart. In doing this, we immerse ourselves in deep contemplation and listen to our inner voice. Our hands are our "second eyes" because of their perceptible sensibility. By putting our hands together, we are concentrating not on the outer world but on our inner world. In this way our energy flows toward the center of our soul.

Each of us has two hands, a right one and a left one. When we use both of them, we can accomplish many more things than when we use only one. Often one hand works actively while the other works passively. Each hand functions independently, yet they can also collaborate with each other. Thus, together the two hands can do various things that a single hand alone cannot achieve.

Our two hands are very similar but are not exactly the same. This is partly because they are symmetrical; however, when we examine them carefully, we note some differences in the form and the length of the fingers as well as in the lines on the palms. They are like fraternal twins of the opposite sex. Yael Haft-Pomrock points out, in her book of chirology, that the hands are opposite and compensatory, and the fewer differences they exhibit, the less conflict there is; at the same time, less conflict means less potential for transformation.[6] It is these differences that may yield the third area in the psyche when we join our hands.

The lines on one's palms relate to one's personality and state of mind and body at the moment. Paracelsus read the lines on the palms of his patients' hands to diagnose their ailments. Haft-Pomrock introduces C. G. Carus's four functions of the hands: the grasping hand (elementary function), the motoric hand, the sensitive hand, and the psychic hand (feeling). She indicates that these functions correspond to the Chinese theory of the hand, in which the grasping function is called the "hand of the Earth," the motoric function is called the "hand of wood," the sensitive function is called the "hand of water," and the psychic hand is called the "hand of metal."[7] This is a metaphor that corresponds to the four elements that make up our world. To join the hands—thus joining these functions—may imply that a person develops direct access to the universe. When we are connected to the great existence far beyond the individual, we may be able to realize the meaning of life and to love others even though we are totally isolated as individuals.

The Hands of the Black Virgin

When I was in my early twenties, I was fascinated by Romanesque art, so I visited many Romanesque churches, mainly in France. As a Japanese person, I felt somewhat uneasy in Gothic churches with their tall spires. However, I instantly felt comfortable in Romanesque churches. I was fascinated by their round arches and the simple carvings that decorate the tympanums and capitals. Something about them may have resonated in my Japanese psyche. In those days I was skeptical about religion, like many Japanese youths of my generation. Having attended a Catholic high school, I had gained some knowledge of Christianity, but I did not believe in it. When I walked into Romanesque churches, however, I felt pensive. I did not realize then why I was so fascinated by them. At that time I did not know that Romanesque churches had been constructed on the sacred places of druidism and that Romanesque art was influenced by Celtic culture. In pre-Roman Celtic society, monks and priests, called "druids," conducted rituals that were related to nature. They especially venerated oak trees and mistletoe. The fundamental purpose of druidic ceremonies was to draw wisdom from nature. Even though the druids were always males, "All the features of druidic thoughts are related to the memories of Mother (feminine, nature), which recurred in the consciousness of sons."[8]

When I walked into the Romanesque churches, I felt the feminine spirituality of the druidic period. In fact, certain similarities have recently come to light between the spiritual climate of Japan and that of Ireland, where the Celtic culture remains even today. The indigenous religion of Japan—Shinto—and druidism both exemplify the deep layers of the psyche. Both religions are forms of nature worship; however, in that no icon of any deity has ever been found, they are not forms of idol worship. Toji Kamata has explained the reason that the spirit of these ancient religions is still alive in these two countries. He says that since both Ireland and Japan have been detached from Eurasia, the spirituality in the depths of the soul—the part that responds to nature—might have survived there.[9]

While I was visiting the Romanesque churches, I was unaware that worship of the Virgin Mary was popular in the twelfth century, when Romanesque art was flourishing. The cult of the Black Virgin was also popular in that same period. The worship of the Blessed Virgin can be regarded as a tradition of feminine spirituality that has faded from popularity today, but its bright side—compassion and purity—

is overemphasized. The Black Virgin, however, still retains all of the feminine strength and power that the ancient goddesses possessed. Because people believed that the Black Virgin performed miracles, they went on pilgrimages to search for figures of her. One such figure is said to be that of the Egyptian Isis, which was brought from the Middle East by the Crusaders. Others are said to have been found by sheer chance, such as one that a shepherd found in a cave, another that turned up in the hollow of a tree, and one that cattle dug up from the ground. Perhaps they are relics of druidic nature worship or are remnants of the Celtic Great Mother Dana worship.

The site where a Black Virgin is enshrined is often thought to be a sacred place of the druids. It is usually characterized by a steep rocky hill, a spring or well, or a special magnetic field formed by a complex of water veins. For instance, one legend says that when people once moved the Black Virgin of Montserrat away from the place where she was discovered, she returned there immediately, so they built a church for her at that spot. Perhaps this is why the Black Virgin is generally enshrined in out-of-the-way places. Rocamadour and Montserrat are on remote rocky hills that must have been very hard to climb in days gone by. It is surprising that despite such a long, steep ascent, pilgrims never ceased to make the journey, which is an indication of their strong faith. Nobility such as Louis XI (1423–1483) were among the earnest pilgrims.

Why did people seek a Black Virgin? The fact that she is enshrined underground—in Chartres, for example—tells us that she is related to the underworld. In other words, the Black Virgin represents the character of the ancient, dark Mother Earth goddess who holds the secret of life and death. While the figure of the Blessed Virgin represents mercy, the Black Virgin has a power that the Virgin Mary does not. It is said that the Black Virgin grants prayers—especially for healing illness or for a successful childbirth. Often she even restores life, according to her devotees. For example, her followers report that she brought a child back to life so that it could be baptized. This trait brings to mind the story of Lilith, who is depicted as Adam's former wife and who left heaven because she would not submit to him.[10]

Though the Black Virgin relates to childbirth, she does not look maternal in the same way as the plump and tender image of Mary that sprang up in the Renaissance period. The Black Virgin of Montserrat, one of the masterpieces of Romanesque carvings, has eyes that are more penetrating than tender. The Black Virgin of Rocamadour is far from beautiful. In spite of the baby Jesus sitting on her knees, her image is by no means maternal. However, she might be an adequate image of feminine spirituality. Perhaps we have been accustomed to the idealized and falsely feminine image for too long.

It is said that the image of the Black Virgin includes not only the Blessed Mary but also Mary Magdalene.[11] This conveys the notion that the Black Virgin is not preoccupied with maternity. In southern France, there is an area where the legend of Mary Magdalene's footsteps and the worship of the Black Virgin overlap. Mary Magdalene, who was a witness to Christ's resurrection, somehow relates to the Black Virgin, who administers life and death.

Regrettably, the Black Mary figure of Rocamadour is missing the fingers, but her slender arms are impressive. The Black Virgin is often characterized by her large hands, which are usually out of proportion to

Figure 3.1. The Underground Chapel for the Black Virgin in the Chartres Cathedral. Photo by Masao Kageyama.

Figure 3.2. The Well in the Underground Chapel of Chartres.
Photo by Masao Kageyama.

her body. I began to consider hands as a symbol of feminine spirituality because I remembered this Black Virgin's big hands. (Tataya Mato has written a beautiful book with drawings of the Black Madonna's hands.[12]) What do the Black Virgin's hands represent? I believe that they represent not only maternity but also the profound wisdom of the feminine nature.

Hands as the Symbol of Feminine Spirituality   *(81)*

Figure 3.3. The Black Virgin in Montserrat. Photo by Masao Kageyama.

Figure 3.4. The Site of Montserrat. Photo by Masao Kageyama.

Figure 3.5. The Black Virgin in Rocamadour, France. Photo by Masao Kageyama.

Figure 3.6. The Site of Rocamadour, France. Photo by Masao Kageyama.

Why is the Black Virgin black? The ecclesiastical explanation is that she has been darkened by the soot of many years of worshipers' candles, but this account seems unsatisfactory. Another one holds that the Black Virgin is a relic of the black stone worship of the ancient Romans, who venerated black meteorites in their worship of the goddess Cybele. Another theory is that she is modeled after suntanned Middle Eastern women in support of the story that the Crusaders took her along on their expeditions. For this explanation, the verse of

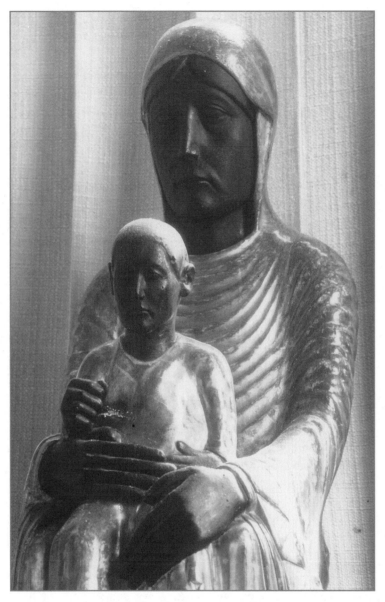

Figure 3.7. The Black Virgin in Marsat (Puy-de-Dome), France.
Photo by Masao Kageyama.

"I am black but beautiful" is always quoted from the Song of Songs (1:5) in the Old Testament. Additionally, the image of the Queen of Sheba sometimes overlaps with the Black Virgin.

When talking about black goddesses, the Indian goddess Kali comes to mind. This terrible deity represents charity and emotion as well as the darkness of the underworld. The black color stands for the Earth, primal chaos, and the *prima materia* of alchemy. It represents a hotbed for seeds, which have limitless potential. Black includes all colors. Munemoto Yanagi, an art historian, explains the color of both the Black Virgin and Kali by the Chinese character 玄 ("gen"). This character means "black," yet not a simple black as in the name of the color; rather, it has philosophical implications. Like the Japanese word 幽玄 ("yuu-gen"), it signifies the profundity that cannot be seen from the outside. Yanagi quotes Lao Tzu's words: "dark-enigma 玄 deep within dark-enigma, gateway of all mystery." This means that darkness yields all wisdom, even though it is too mysterious to be understood. Lao Tzu also says, "The valley spirit never dies. It's called 'dark female-enigma.'" Here the dark female enigma signifies the source of everything. Yanagi defines "gen" as being "more than sensational black or invisible darkness, therefore we are unable to recognize it mentally. Thus 'gen' is the source beyond time and space." Yanagi also says, " 玄 (gen) is the darkness which transcends light and darkness. It is the mother of existence and nothingness, and the darkness far across life and death."[13] He maintains that the blackness of the Black Virgin is both the source of everything and the color of the highest virtue.

Thus, we can say that, through her color, the Black Virgin represents profound feminine wisdom. Moreover, her large hands may be the important symbol that we have left behind.

The Hands of the Kannon

Many people have made pilgrimages in order to worship the Black Virgin. There were four main routes leading to Santiago de Compostela, and pilgrims were able to pay homage to the Black Virgin at various stops along the way. The starting points for these roads were Paris, Vézelay, Le Puy, and Arles. The basilica at Vézelay is purported to contain the relics of Mary Magdalene, and Le Puy is an important center of Black Virgin worship. There are pilgrimage routes in Japan, too. Along one of the most popular roads, there are thirty-three different temples that people can stop at and visit while praying to the Kannon bosatsu. This particular route became popular in the eleventh and twelfth centuries and gradually spread throughout the country. Even today, people still set out on these pilgrimages.

In Buddhism, a *bosatsu,* or bodhisattva, is similar to a *nyorai* (Buddha) or *tathagata* (an enlightened one). The difference between them is that, in order to save human beings in this karmic world, the bosatsu purposely and compassionately stays slightly short of enlightenment, or becoming a nyorai. The bosatsu occupies a position between human beings and the nyorai and acts as an intermediary between them. There are many different types of bosatsu, but perhaps the most beloved is the one called Kannon, or Avalokitésvara. The Kannon bosatsu is said to be related to the Hindu god Shiva or to come from the great Earth Mother worship of the Middle East. A protean change of the figure is characteristic of the Kannon. This bosatsu saves people from hardships such as illness. Moreover, with the spread of Jodo Buddhism, the Kannon came to grant people's prayers to go to Jodo (Pure Land or the land of Perfect Bliss) after death as an assistant to Amitabba or Amida Nyorai. The name Kannon, meaning "to see" or "to recognize sounds," comes from the fact that it keeps its eyes on people so as not to miss the slightest appeal or groan of suffering. Interestingly, the name Mary also means "seer."

Kannon worship was at first quite popular in China, and it accompanied Buddhism to Japan in the sixth century. The Kannon's great appeal is, in short, mercy, and its followers believe in and worship it ardently. Originally, a bosatsu, as well as Buddha, is regarded as something that goes beyond gender. A bosatsu is neither male nor female. Even so, the Kannon has a feminine aspect, which might reflect the fact that its origin was a Mother Earth goddess in the Middle East. Moreover, its merciful quality evokes a maternal image. In fact, its statues often take on a feminine appearance. I think that Kannon worship may be a response to people's needs for feminine spirituality.

Especially in Japan, the feminine element of Kannon grew stronger as it became mixed with the goddess worship prevalent in ancient Shinto. As I mentioned previously, Shintoism did not involve idols, but once syncretism with Buddhism occurred, people began to see the images of goddesses through Buddhist figures.

The Kannon bosatsu is depicted by various figures. Senju Kannon, or Sahasrabhuja, is one of them. This name means "Kannon with a thousand hands or arms," which is clearly a direct influence of Hinduism in India. Although Buddha figures with many hands are not rare, only the Kannon figure has a thousand hands. Senju Kannon, as well as other kinds of Kannon, was first worshipped in China and then brought to Japan. In the beginning, Kannon worship included a strong desire for worldly gain. Then, in the eleventh and twelfth centuries, opposition to the secularization of Buddhism led to the combining of Kannon worship with Shugendo, a kind of religious practice in which the followers seek truth by living an austere life close to nature. Thus, people enshrined the Kannon bosatsu at sacred places for the Shugendo practitioners throughout the countryside, and followers began to make pilgrimages. Most of these sacred places are found beside the ocean, lakes, or springs or next to trees in the mountains, where nature's energy is apparent. Because Senju Kannon is worshipped in these places, I believe that it holds a special meaning for the Japanese people. Although the Kannon worship was imported to Japan, the combination of Kannon worship and Shugendo and the pilgrimages takes place only in Japan and does not occur in India or China. The reason for this is that Shugendo itself is a combination of Japanese indigenous nature worship and esoteric Buddhism. When I think of the European pilgrimages to worship the Black Virgin and the visits to the sacred places of the druids, I find some similarities between them and the pilgrimages to worship the Kannon.

As mentioned earlier, the Senju Kannon is the Kannon bosatsu with a thousand hands. A thousand, or "sen" in Japanese, represents a very large number. Usually this figure is made with 2 hands joined together and with 40 hands holding various objects that symbolize the particular power of the Kannon. Followers believe that each hand has the power to save all living things from the 25 worlds of delusions. Since 25 times 40 hands equals 1,000 hands, then at least 42 hands need to be created for a Senju Kannon figure. In rare cases, 1,000 hands were actually made for the figure, only two examples of which are well known in Japan today. One is in Toshodaiji in Nara, and the other is in Fujidera in Osaka.

Another characteristic of the Senju Kannon is that it has many faces on the top of its head, and each face has a different expression. Usually this Kannon—called the Juichimen Kannon—has eleven faces. The name means "one that looks everywhere." At the center of the top of the statue, there is a nyorai, or Buddha face. There are three "mercy faces" at the front around the nyorai face, three angry faces at the left side, three beastly faces at the right side, and one hateful face laughing boisterously in the back. Sometimes tender, sometimes scolding, and sometimes playful, the faces guide people to salvation or enlightenment.

The Kannon bosatsu is the embodiment of the Daiji-daihi-nyorai, or the Buddha of great mercy. Among the various Kannon bosatsu, the Senju Kannon is believed to be able to perform miracles, such as extending life, atoning for people's sins, driving illness away, and fulfilling wishes. Perhaps Senju Kannon was created in order for people to depend upon it and to act as a channel for their desires. Moreover, the Kannon bosatsu is said to transform itself into various disguises in order to save people. According to Buddhist sutras, it can transform itself into thirty-three different figures or forms, such as a tree or an herb.

What do the thousand hands of Senju Kannon represent? According to Buddhist teachings, they indicate the Kannon's merciful nature and desire to save people. Each object that the Kannon holds in its hands symbolizes its merit. If you look closely at these items, you will notice that they originally belonged to other bosatsu, or Myo-o (vidya-raya: apotheosized people with immense spiritual wisdom). For example, among these objects are the shakujo (scepter) and houju (jewel ball) that belong to the Jizo bosatsu. Therefore, the Senju Kannon likely has the attributes of the Jizo or Ksitigarbha, too. The Jizo bosatsu is probably just as popular as the Kannon is. Even now, people worship the Jizo as the protector of children. It is said that Jizo was originally a great Earth Mother in the Middle East, and followers believe that it goes back and forth between this world and the underworld. Like the Black Virgin, who revived a dead child who had not yet been baptized, Jizo protects deceased children from falling into hell. Though there is a tale in India that Jizo's precursor was a female, in Japan the Jizo has never had a feminine aspect, unlike Kannon, which has a rather feminine appearance. Instead, the Jizo assumes the figure of a young Buddhist monk. Among the various Kannon bosatsu, the Senju Kannon is thought to have a special power to perform good deeds, such as extending life, atoning for people's sins, driving illness away, and fulfilling wishes.

Senju Kannon's formal name is Senju Sengen Kannon, which means "Kannon with a thousand hands and a thousand eyes." This is because each hand also has an eye. While the hands represent salvation, I feel that the eyes, which can be taken as a symbol of feminine spirituality, indicate more than maternal mercy. When you look at the Senju Kannon at Toshodaiji temple, most of the hands seem to spread out like beams of light. However, they remind me of Medusa, whose snake hair may be a similar symbol of feminine wisdom.

As mentioned earlier, many of the places for Senju Kannon worship are located near water, just as for the Black Virgin. This signifies that the Senju Kannon is connected with feminine spirituality in a way similar to the Black Virgin. Kiyomizu Temple ("temple of pure water") in Kyoto is a typical example of Senju Kannon worship. When followers go there, they grip the strings that are tied to the Senju Kannon's hands as if to receive power from the statue. Moreover, there are many tales that recount the miraculous deeds of Senju Kannon. In the *Konjaku Monogatari,* one of the largest selections of ancient Japanese folk tales, some of the variations describe how a strange woman saved another woman who was facing certain difficulties. Later, this strange woman was discovered to be a transformed Senju Kannon whom the saved woman usually worshipped. Also, in many other tales about Kannon's miracles, the Kannon transforms into a female in order to save people. According to *Reigenki,* or folk tales about miracles, at the Hase temple, which is a popular place for Kannon pilgrimages, the Kannon is said to have declared that "only a female can save people

Figure 3.8. Senju Kannon Images in Toshodaiji, Eighth Century.
Photo by Kozo Ogawa (Asukaen).

with ferocious hearts in this world. From now on, I am going to be in-carnated as a female so as to guard the country and save the people."[14] This statement is rather curious because, according to a well-known Buddhist doctrine, a female's soul cannot rest in peace or attain en-lightenment without first transforming into a male.

Similar to the Virgin Mary, the Kannon's image generally tends to be quite bright, which may symbolize idealized maternity. The similarity between the Virgin Mary and the Kannon is expressed in the fact that when Christianity came to Japan and was subsequently forbidden to be practiced (for about three hundred years, beginning at the end of the sixteenth century), Christians would covertly pray to the figure of "Mary Kannon." Even so, the Senju Kannon is not only bright but also evokes awe by its unusual appearance.

It was mainly the nobility that sought the mercy of the Kannon, and they preferred the Sei Kannon, the one with the simple, tender face and without numerous hands and faces. On the other hand, most ordinary people prayed to the Senju Kannon for protection from misfortune rather than for mercy. The many weapons that are held in its hands suggest such power. Senju Kannon's belongings, which come from the Jizo bosatsu, or Fudo-Myo-ou (Acalanatha), also imply that its underworld aspect and never-flinching, angry character come from the Jizo bosatsu and Fudo-Myo-ou. Thus, the fact that Senju Kannon embodies the elements of both heavenly brightness and the darkness of the underworld shows that this Kannon has an ambivalent nature, like that of the great Earth Mother.

Both the Black Virgin worship in Europe and the Senju Kannon worship in Japan represent people's desire for feminine spirituality. It is interesting that both forms of worship are characterized by hands and pilgrimages. Both are on the periphery of the framework of Christianity and Buddhism, and both place great importance on the power of nature. Despite the cultural differences between Europe and Japan, there flows something common underneath—feminine spirituality.

There is another interesting commonality, also. The expansion of the worship of the Virgin Mary in Europe in the twelfth and thirteenth centuries is said to be related to the fact that, in the Christian world at that time, apocalyptic eschatology was spreading, and there was much talk of the "Last Judgment." At that time, the Mendicant Monks preached fearful tales about what would happen if one went to hell. Frightened people threw themselves on the Virgin Mary, and worship of her expanded. Almost at the same time, Mappo-shiso ("thought of Mappo") spread throughout Japan. Mappo, or the latter days, refers to the last days of existence, a time when people cannot

Figure 3.9. Detail of the Senju Kannon Images in Toshodaiji.
Photo by Kozo Ogawa (Asukaen).

achieve enlightenment no matter how hard they try. This teaching says that people will spend eternity in hell. Buddhist monks depicted the awful scene of hell in graphic terms. Thus people begged the Jizo bosatsu for salvation, and Jizo worship has thrived ever since.

As I mentioned earlier, the Jizo was originally a Middle Eastern Earth goddess that was incorporated into Buddhism. Occasionally, the Jizo would travel to hell and negotiate with its ruler, the Enma-daio, to save people. It is even said that Jizo and Enma-daio are the same character. Thus, it is curious that in Europe and Japan, which are so far apart, people similarly feared hell and searched for salvation—for something that embodied feminine spirituality. Despite the cultural and religious differences between the countries, such synchronistic events may be evidence of Jung's collective unconscious. Moreover, these events show us that people from different cultures may be able to understand each other in the depths of their psyches. In this regard, it is significant that feminine spirituality is the bridge that connects them.

We can also view the Islamic world's "hand of Fatima" as a charm that protects people from evil. Fatima, the mother of the prophets, who is also venerated as the Virgin or the Great Maryam, bears the traits of creative Sophia.

Sanju-sangen-do temple in Kyoto is famous for its one thousand Senju Kannon figures lined up on the sides of the main Kannon figure. Each statue has forty-two hands. The view is glorious, and the long building is filled with spiritual energy. The numerous hands inside this temple inspire us to contemplate the particular meaning of hands. Doing so may awaken various powers that are asleep in the depths of our psyche.

About Maternity

How to deal with feminine spirituality and maternity is a difficult issue because the history of praise for maternity has been confused with feminine spirituality. To bear and raise children is indeed an important function, but that is just one element of women's spirituality. However, childbearing and the rearing of children are the only matters for which men must depend upon women. Thus, these are

Figure 3.10. A Thousand Senju Kannon Images in Sanjusangendo.
Photo by Kozo Ogawa (Asukaen).

the only aspects of women that have been valued. Also, women themselves have fostered such praise for maternity because they realize that it is the single area in which they are respected and appreciated. In other words, women have been tethered by maternity.

However, maternity sometimes prevents women from awakening to themselves. Of course, devoting oneself to the care of others is a worthy endeavor, as in the case of motherhood. Even so, it is unfortunate that such a virtue has been attributed to and required only of women. Not everybody can be a Mother Teresa. Hence, women feel guilty when they cannot become an ideal mother, and they blame themselves or unconsciously turn negative and ultimately hurt their children or other people. Consequently, they sometimes control their children and husbands and even abuse the former. To avoid such situations, women must put maternity aside for a while and think about their feminine nature.

Both the Black Virgin and the Senju Kannon have certain powers that cannot be explained only by maternity. The aspect of maternity or mercy is usually emphasized when considering the Blessed Virgin Mary and the Kannon bosatsu. However, people have prayed to the Black Virgin or Senju Kannon for many other things as well, such as wisdom, an understanding of nature, strength, a keen eye for truth, and the ability to administer life and death. The powers of the Black Mary and Senju Kannon emanate from their connection with the Earth and even the underworld.

Women have lost sight of those elements somewhere in themselves. They willingly apply the images of tenderness and acceptance, like the Virgin Mary or Kannon, to themselves. On the other hand, they have at times assumed the image of a witch or an evil woman. Hereafter, however, women must also contemplate and recognize their internal negative power and account for it. By doing so, they can make good use of it. In reality, it is rather easy to live according to men's expectations, and women have tended to take advantage of this. No one is to blame for doing so. For women to reacquire their feminine spirituality, they must free themselves from the illusions that men have imposed on them and descend from the position of goddess to the Earth as a human being—it does not mean to swing from a holy woman to a witch, but rather to face and become one's real self.

It is also important to question the well-known female qualities that males have defined, for example, the tendency to accept everything as feminine nature, or connecting with others, or the so-called Eros. Indeed, these are important elements for everyone, but they are not exclusively feminine in nature. In order for a woman to determine her own destiny, she also needs assertiveness and verbalization skills. With the inclusion of those elements, I would like to further examine feminine spirituality. In other words, through feminine spirituality, women may consider themselves as both a sensitive receiver and a transmitter. Both the Virgin Mary and the Kannon include the characteristics of seeing or watching. Thus, the ability to see essential things is one of the important aspects of feminine spirituality.

I have been discussing the hand as a symbol of feminine spirituality, but clearly we have *two* hands. Not only do these two hands work as cooperative partners so as to make the impossible possible, but they also respond to each other. Perhaps we have much hidden potential in the interspaces between our hands. The Senju Kannon of Fujiidera temple, whose hands are slightly apart, prompts us to reflect on the infinite possibility between the two hands. In Egyptian hieroglyphics, the vital energy of the spirit "kah" is symbolized by two raised hands. What is more, our two hands connect to the brother-sister archetype,

Figure 3.11. Senju Kannon Images in Fujiidera, Eighth Century.
Fujiidera Temple, Osaka.

Hands as the Symbol of Feminine Spirituality (97)

which is hidden deep in our psyche and makes the impossible possible. Two hands applaud, as Anne Sexton beautifully describes in her poem "Two Hands."[15] Perhaps we should place more trust not only in our heads and hearts but also in our hands.

Hands and Language

According to Thomas Aquinas, if human beings had walked on four legs, they could not have used their hands, and language would never have evolved.[16] As I mentioned before, our hands separate us from other animals. So do the words we use. What sort of relationship exists between our hands and language? Sign language shows that the movement of the hands may serve for communication just as well as spoken and written words. Sign language includes symbolism and movement. In addition, certain movements of the hands have particular implications that are evident in various types of communication and in some religious rituals; for instance, when people pray or chant the sutras of esoteric Buddhism, they fold their hands and fingers in various forms or shapes.

In considering the hand as the symbol of feminine spirituality, it may be important to contemplate the significance that words and language have for women. Perhaps women should use a form of language that has an important connection with the hand. We may have to use something beyond the tongue and head when composing or communicating. For example, the more a newborn baby learns to use its hands, the better is its ability to speak words. By using their hands, babies learn about their environment while developing relationships with others and identifying themselves. Perhaps words themselves were once intrinsically connected to our internal nature. Consider the meaning of the term "mother tongue." However, as we mature, language recedes from our internal nature. As a result, we become suspicious of the words we use. Consequently, the more we try to compensate for this, the more argumentative we become.

Intrinsically speaking, words awaken images. However, the more argumentative or logical we become, the more superficial words become. On the other hand, a scientific thesis has to be argumentative (logical) so as not to be misunderstood. This might be a mixed blessing that brings women serious problems. Women have learned to use abstract words by training, and they have taught themselves to compose their thoughts logically. Nevertheless, this causes women to disassociate from themselves, with the result that they feel somewhat different or even uncomfortable. Women need to get their own words and language back.

Pascal Quinard tells us that, when he was a child, he used to see his mother's face look like Medusa's death mask—when her words were on the tip of her tongue but would not come out. He says, "Fathers deliver the names which have no meaning by themselves. They force the language on children. Women, crying with pain, transfer the load of death to the shoulders of newborn babies. They deliver the origin. Fathers deliver the names. Mothers deliver the cries."[17] Perhaps we have to recall the words connected with the hands and tongues of mothers.

Hands Know

Sometimes we drop into deep thought and come almost to a standstill. The next time this happens to you, let your hands write or draw something in a notebook, and you might find something unexpected. Jung says, "If there is a high degree of conscious cramp, often only the hands are capable of fantasy; they model or draw figures that are sometimes quite foreign to the conscious mind."[18] He means that the hands have a certain autonomy. When we see our hands writing or drawing—or the result of their actions—we recognize something afresh and see what we have not been able to see before. Often it is the hands that serve to connect the consciousness and the unconsciousness.

Ancient people used their hands to do everything. They even used them to sew their clothes stitch by stitch. Today, because we can buy most things with money, few people have to make their clothes themselves. Moreover, we can do many things by simply pushing a button. Indeed, this is a sign of civilization. But, in gradually using our hands less and less, we may be overlooking something important. Perhaps by not using our hands, our psyches have become increasingly insensitive.

Figure 3.12. An Expression of Sand Play. Anonymous. Photo by Sonoko Toyoda.

This is the reason I emphasize creative activities in order to restore feminine spirituality. The hands can express things that are springing up from deep within us. Of course, not all of us can be artists or writers. If we wish to be, we will need much training. This is not what I am asking you to do, however. I think we should exercise our creativity in order to learn our true identity. For example, we could begin by doing housework differently from the way we normally do. The hands are powerful friends, and we must recognize this and seek our potential in order to be free from the restrictions with which we have bound ourselves.

One point of view holds that it is unnecessary to make forms as long as someone is creative. It is said that men search for material forms, whereas women do not. Indeed, seeking only concrete objects is a problem. Nonetheless, I think it is necessary for today's women to create shapes in some manner because we can often pull something into our consciousness only after creating a visual image of it. I would recommend sand play, as begun by Dora Kalff, as one convenient means of playing creatively. It is easy to touch sand and to draw or put favorite figures in it, and most people are content with their sand tray after they have created something there. Many people say that their compositions are completely different from what they expected, but even so they are quite satisfied with them. The visual images expressed in the trays awaken us to our own internal world again. They are sometimes even more meaningful than our dreams. The images we create enable us to express something that we cannot convey in words. Moreover, visualization encourages the composer to continue to progress. Indeed, sand play becomes more significant when a therapist is present, but, even without a counselor, simply using the hands in sand play brings its own merit.

The hands are aware of more than what we are conscious of. When you get lost, you may ask your hands to show you the way.

CHAPTER 4

How to Recover Our Lost Hands

I hope by now you have expanded your image of hands. Thus far I have taken hands as a symbol of feminine spirituality. I know this concept is a bit challenging because hands—as a very important part of the human body—have already been described as symbols of many other things. For example, they signify activity, power, and control, and in this sense they are also a symbol of a leader. These meanings center especially on the right hand and represent the will of God, which is often depicted as a big hand reaching down from a cloud in the sky. Sometimes the right hand signifies the consciousness, and the left hand, the unconscious. My point is that we need *both* hands to represent feminine spirituality.

Although it might be somewhat audacious to consider hands as a symbol of feminine spirituality, I do so because feminine spirituality is as important and indispensable for humans as the hands are. What I regard as feminine spirituality is something that operates in accordance with nature and the universe, a kind of transcendent wisdom that we cannot grasp by rational thinking and which bridges two opposite things. It is also a kind of insight that sees through the essence of a phenomenon and pulls meaning from it.

I believe feminine spirituality is indispensable for humans, and, because it is deeply rooted in our lives, at one time people must have been aware of it. We cannot understand ourselves only with our rational mind. To understand and accept ourselves, we need something transcendent. Religions have helped us in our attempt to understand and accept ourselves. Yet, I think women, from their very nature, must have had this ability to grasp the true meaning of things not in a rational way but through insight. At least they have been more insightful than men.

The patriarchal world has found this characteristic of women unacceptable because believers in the rational mind do not accept things that are inexplicable in a rational manner, and they even feel terrified of and threatened by them. This trait of women has been denied, neglected, and rejected, with the result that women themselves have come to disbelieve this essential quality. Instead, they have tried to reshape themselves in the feminine image that men have of them. In order to live in that male-imposed framework, women find they have to eradicate the "nuisance" or "bothersome" aspects of their personality. This is what has happened with women's hands. Women have even been willing to have their hands cut off to be accepted in the men's world. Remember the story of "The Handless Maiden" with this context in mind.

However, I believe the memories of our lost hands are still somewhere deep within our psyches. Moreover, some remnants of feminine spirituality are still evident in various cultures around the world. As stated earlier, there are vestiges of it in the Okinawan culture as well as in the pilgrimages to the Black Virgins in Europe and those to the Senju Kannon in Japan. What we should do now is to take off the veil of Eros for a while and go back to the starting point of life in order to be alone and examine the depths of our psyches. Then we should try to draw closer to us the memories we find there.

This is not an easy task. In the first place, it is difficult to be alone. One reason is that, for a long time, women have defined themselves only within the context of their connections with other people. It is difficult to liberate oneself from such a dependent situation. When you love someone, or you want someone to love you, or when you criticize or attack someone, you depend on that person. The more uncertain you are of yourself, the more such a tendency occurs, and you find it necessary to stick to other people. It is not easy to find a way out of this vicious circle.

In the past, feminine spirituality may have been transmitted from mothers to daughters in the feminine lineage. Possibly it is still transmitted that way in "happy" or "healthy" families. However, in most cases, mothers of the past two or three generations have not passed it on to their daughters. If mothers have already been influenced by the masculine sense of values, their daughters do not inherit feminine spirituality from them. Such mothers cannot develop their creativity, and their unlived or nonmanifested creativeness becomes a sort of subliminal negative force that rubs their children the wrong way. Especially if the child is a daughter, the mother identifies with her and tries to live through her. This mother will therefore have many expectations of her daughter. Yet, at the same time, she is quite envious in her deeper psyche because her daughter has potential that the mother lacks. In this way, relationships between mothers and daughters have worsened.

In many civilized countries it is fairly common nowadays to encounter girls who suffer from eating disorders. Some of these cases result from rigid dieting. However, many women want to have a slender figure because they are pursuing the slim figure that men idealize. Such self-destructive dieting is connected with the metaphor of cutting off one's hands. In eating disorders, many girls repeat binge eating and vomiting in almost a ritual way, and they are actually starving themselves. They stuff themselves with an enormous amount of food and then vomit it all. Why? Food does not stave off their hunger, and it is not food that they are craving. It seems to me that these girls are craving feminine spirituality. They cannot get it from their mothers, just as their mothers were also unable to get it from their mothers. Thus their psyche develops a black void—a feeling of emptiness. These women cannot feel secure in themselves, and although they work hard at everything they do, they have no self-confidence.

Daughters often have a grudge against their mothers because the latter are unable to provide the right spiritual food for them. However, we must realize that a mother cannot give her daughter what she herself does not have. So what should we do? If you seek what you lack in the outer world, no one will be able to give it to you. It simply cannot be found there. I think each woman should look deep inside and reach for the old memories that are still in the depth of her soul. Women need to regain the hands that they have unknowingly lost. What can be done to achieve this objective? Women must engage in creative activities. For a very long time they have had no opportunity to express themselves. Unless they acted like men or sold their souls to men, they were not allowed to act creatively.

In Japan, the Heian period (from the eighth through the thirteenth centuries) is well known as the era of women's culture. At that time many women writers appeared, and they wrote many stories and essays. The most renowned author is Murasaki-Shikibu, who wrote "The Tale of Genji." These women writers were perhaps the mainstay of the Heian culture. Unfortunately, Japanese history has not experienced a similar era since that time. One thing we should not forget is that those women authors wrote in a manner that was different from the way men wrote. In those days men wrote using only Chinese characters called kanji. This was the acceptable way to write at that time. But women writers wrote without using kanji; instead, they used simpler letters called kana. This does not mean that the women did not know how to use kanji. It is said that Murasaki-Shikibu was so intelligent that she could use kanji perfectly. Nevertheless, she chose not to use them when she wrote a story. Why? Writing in kana was probably more suitable for her to express herself. Gradually this kana writing was commonly accepted and became the foundation of the Japanese cultural tradition. This demonstrates that the Japanese culture has a feminine basis. After the Heian period, however, more men than women began to take an active part in Japanese culture. This is a pity. Now each woman has to find her own manner of self-expression.

Psychotherapy and Feminine Spirituality

When one of my clients realized her dependence on men, she once said, "I seem to be eager to move my hands although I have lost them. Maybe I have to admit that I have lost them all by myself." She was dependent on men, and at the same time she had a deep hatred for them. She had so many expectations of men that she always felt betrayed by them. She wanted them to become her hands, but they could never become hands that were an integral part of her own life. Thus those hands were never able to satisfy her. As I said earlier, if a woman wants to regain her lost hands, she should seek them neither in the outer world nor in other people, but she should descend to the depth of her own spirit. Psychotherapy can be very helpful in this task.

I think psychotherapy itself is a kind of *temenos*—a place for reflection—where feminine spirituality operates. C. G. Jung saw alchemy as a model of the individuation process in psychotherapy. In alchemy, the aim of the process is symbolized as the sacred marriage of the sun and the moon and of the king and queen. The latter marriage is understood as the marriage of Apollo and Diana, in other words, a brother-sister marriage. Jung points out that the image of this sacred marriage is the projection of the relationship between the alchemist (the adept) and the mystic sister *(soror mystica)* who attend the alchemical process. We do not have enough information about how the mystic sister contributes to the whole process, but I presume that her presence is important. The fact that this female figure is a sister—and not a mother or a wife—is meaningful.

As I stated earlier, in Okinawa it is believed that women have spiritual power that men do not have, and a sister is regarded as a guardian spirit for her brother. Japan may have had the same tradition in ancient times because Okinawa and mainland Japan shared the same culture until the sixth century. Okinawa, however, has retained this tradition, whereas Japan has lost it. Kunio Yanagida, a Japanese ethnologist, calls this spiritual quality of women "the sister's power."

When I think of the mystic sister of alchemy, this notion of the sister's power comes to mind. The reason the partner of the adept is a sister—rather than a mother or a wife—seems clear to me. The brother-sister relationship has a special meaning that is absent in the other male-female relationships. That is, a brother and a sister are opposite as a man and a woman, but they have the same basis because they are born from the same parents, so they are different and equal at the same time. Accordingly, in a brother-sister relationship one does not overpower the other, and the two are totally equal. A brother-sister marriage would be sacred because it is taboo and thus impossible, and because it is impossible, it has symbolic meaning.

Unfortunately, Jung did not focus on the fact that a brother and a sister are equal. He was interested only in the opposite qualities of a man and a woman and in the incest motif. This is why he talks about mother-son incest as well as brother-sister incest from this image of the sacred marriage. In this sense Robert Stein points out the crucial meaning of the brother-sister relationship. Still, he overemphasizes the incest issue as a kind of sexual fact. As in alchemy, I prefer to take this sacred marriage motif much more symbolically. I think it is not the point that we project too much reality onto the symbolic images of alchemy. If alchemy is compared with psychotherapy, what do the adept and the mystic sister represent in psychotherapy? Is the adept an analyst? His erudition authorizes him to play this role. Who controls the fire and watches for slight changes in the retorts? Maybe not only the adept but also the mystic sister is at work. I presume that the mystic sister's presence has something to do with feminine spirituality, and in this sense the analyst's role is closer to that of the mystic sister than to the adept. Or the adept-sister pair might together constellate feminine spirituality. In any event, I believe feminine spirituality is crucial in psychotherapy.

I say this because psychotherapy itself is creative work. In order to accept the contradictory situation as it is and find a new way without denying both sides, we need transcendent wisdom. All of us must seek our own unique way without imitating any models. If we want something new to come forth, we need the third sphere—where the unconscious relates to the consciousness, where the inner world relates to the outer world, where one relates to the other, and where the sky relates to the Earth. In this realm, one is two, and two are one. This is the way feminine spirituality works. Moreover, this creative process itself can be a route by which to recover feminine spirituality.

Beautifully describing the wild-woman archetype, Clarissa Pinkola Estés says that women need to recover their wild nature, which they have lost. "When women reassert their relationship with the wildish nature, they are gifted with a permanent and internal watcher, a knower, a visionary, an oracle, an inspiratrice, an intuitive, a maker, a creator, and a listener who guide, suggest, and urge vibrant life in the inner and outer worlds." She also emphasizes the creativity of women:

"[A] woman's creative ability is her most valuable asset, for it gives outwardly and it feeds her inwardly at every level: psychic, spiritual, mental, emotive and economic."[1]

As James Hillman says, "We are cured when we are no longer only masculine in psyche, no matter whether we are male or female in biology. . . . The end of analysis coincides with the acceptance of femininity."[2] This process of recovering feminine spirituality is important for both men and women. Men need to overcome their deep-seated fear of the feminine. Conquering this fear is not similar to killing a dragon in order to rescue a princess as was once thought. Instead men need to ask the dragon for her wisdom. For a woman who wishes to acquire a sense of herself, recovering her feminine spirituality is crucial because it is her essential quality. Maybe she needs to take off the dress of a princess and go out and tame the dragon.

Equality in relationships between men and women and also between an analyst and an analysand is desirable. To attain this, we would do well to follow the brother-sister relationship model. With this type of arrangement, an analyst and an analysand can avoid a muddy transference situation, although they still feel connected to each other in the deeper layers of the psyche. I think when feminine spirituality works, the brother-sister archetype is constellated, and vice versa.

Obstacles to Feminine Creativity

For a long time, women have expended their energy mainly for other people. It is much easier for them to use it for other people than for themselves. They get into the habit of doing this. If they place their priorities on themselves, they feel first selfish and then guilty. Needless to say, it is admirable to help others. However, if you do this and at the same time neglect your own needs, you will lose yourself, and you will need *others* to support *you*. In this case, you are sacrificing yourself and demanding recompense or gratitude from others at the same time. This situation sometimes happens between a "perfect" mother and her child. If you really want to help other people, you have to live your own life. Otherwise you make those whom you have helped feel burdened. In order to feel full of life, you need to put your energy into yourself and be creative.

What are the obstacles to a woman's creativity? You might count some outer conditions as barriers, but they are not as daunting as those inside you. I think the main obstacles are fear, resignation, anxiety, and self-doubt. Women are intimidated by being evaluated by men's standards. They are not used to communicating freely and honestly. Moreover, they are afraid that their ideas will be rejected or ignored in the masculine, opinionated world if they even dare to express themselves. However, if women communicate in order to be accepted in the men's world and if they succeed in attaining a certain level of approval, they will still not be satisfied because this sort of success is not a part of their true nature. This fear also makes them worry about keeping up their physical appearance.

To be born as a woman in this man's world evokes a certain sense of resignation. Women continuously learn this because, everywhere they turn, they come across social and mental restrictions. Thus women tend to be resigned from the beginning—before they even try. On the other hand, the social expectations to be a good wife and a good mother for their families are, from childhood, hammered into their heads. This alone might make them draw back from the challenge of self-expression, considering the heavy pressure to conform to society's expectations. Women's anxiety and self-doubt are interconnected. Whenever we try to pursue our creativity, we hear a voice inside us that says, "What you are doing is completely absurd, useless, and pointless. It has no meaning. You can never accomplish it. You are not able to do it." And so on. This is the inner, negative "father's voice" that we have incorporated since our birth. And this self-doubt evokes tremendous anxiety when girls develop into women.

I think, however, the biggest obstacle of all might be the fact that women always have a way out—an escape. Women have many social and mental restrictions that bind and suffocate them. But women, too, use these restrictions as a pretext for not realizing their creativity. They believe that they are not responsible for doing nothing; rather, it is the restrictions that are responsible, they tell themselves. I think we must admit that women benefit from the restrictions (for example, our social system and familial binds) in a sense by not facing their own laziness. There are many types of escape that women can resort to. For some women, the care of children is a way out, and for other women, supporting their husband is an escape.

Of course, women need tremendous energy if they try to cultivate their own way in the face of these restrictions. Sometimes women clash with the people around them, so it is understandable that they tend to avoid pursuing their creative talents. However, if women continue to look for a way out, they will always be dissatisfied with themselves and envious of others. Moreover, a woman's unexplored creativity tends both to become a kind of negative force in the unconscious and to offend others even without her knowing it. Jung believed that creativity is one of the most basic of human instincts, just like hunger and sexual desire. People cannot live without it. However, women, who are destined to be biologically creative, that is, to give birth to a child, might themselves come to believe that they do not have this craving for inventiveness except by becoming a mother. Sometimes women cling to their children as if they are the only proof of their resourcefulness.

Abandonment of Creativity

It is true that bearing children and raising them give women incomparable experiences and great joys. It is encouraging for mothers to watch their children's growth. In this sense, children raise their mothers, too. However, if people were born with a vocation, that is, with a certain, individual purpose in life, it would be strange to think that all women were born in order to bear and raise children. It is more natural to think that everyone, including women, is born with a meaning to live apart from their biological assignment. Nevertheless, there is still a general belief that women become authentic only through the experience of childbearing. Women who are infertile or have no chance to conceive feel ashamed and seek every possible means of having a child, even to the extent of trying artificial insemination.

On the other hand, a woman can choose to abort her conceived child. Eva Pattis Zoja takes up the problem of abortion from a new perspective. She regards abortion as a sort of first step in which a woman initially denies the motherhood that has overly controlled her and then attains independence as a woman.[3] Certainly there are some women who begin to reflect meaningfully on themselves after their painful experience with abortion. Still, it is difficult to generalize these cases. There are also some women who abort their children because they are too young, or they do not want to give up their occupations, or perhaps they abort just for the sake of their reputation and even their physical appearance. In such cases most of these women do not feel guilty, at least at the conscious level. Unconsciously, however, they are tied to this incident, and when conditions are more favorable later in their lives, they may become obsessed with having children as a reaction to their earlier abortion. Women who have undergone an abortion also suffer from their loss and not infrequently become depressed.

One of my analysands had had several abortions. It was difficult for me to understand how such a thing could be repeated so many times. She said that she did not have any guilty feelings, but her body and mind were undoubtedly troubled. When we talked about it, she finally admitted that her repeated abortions might have been a sort of dilatory suicide. To kill a conceived child before it comes in the world seems to me to be the abandonment of creativity. James Hillman says, "As an interior drama the aborted child is the miscarriage of the archetypal qualities we have presented: hope for the future, the sense of conquest, the new start and fulfilled end. The dead child is our lost hope and failed spark, our creative disappointment and stricken imagination that can point no way forward, spontaneity, openness, movement gone."[4] This analysand kept herself alive by helping other people. Without this devotion to others, she felt insecure. She once said, "I am a mother to everyone, so I don't need to have my own child." I think there are many women like this, that is, women who sacrifice themselves to serve others and who give up their own creativity. Now I understand this analysand's repeated abortions as symbolic suicides, all the while verifying her procreative capacity.

Pattis Zoja explains abortion as women's first step in liberating themselves from the maternal bind. This schema, however, resembles that of men's liberation from their mother's domination by rejecting the mother, which is symbolized as a dragon conquest. However, David Tacy points out that this schema evokes some problems for men, too. He says that men lose the connection with feminine spirituality by slaying the dragon, and this loss causes them to suffer enormously in the real world.[5] As I mentioned earlier, the loss of feminine spirituality is devastating for both women and men because they cannot connect to their true nature without it.

To reiterate, we need to put aside the maternal issue when we think of feminine spirituality. Nevertheless, this does not mean that I deny the maternal quality in the feminine psyche. It is a component of feminine spirituality. I think the heritage of feminine spirituality must be transferred from mothers to daughters in a natural way, so I differ here with Pattis Zoja. I especially do not agree with her when she posits Athena as a symbol of feminine spirituality. Athena is a typical father's daughter, and her wisdom is favorable for men and is not authentic feminine wisdom. Although a threatening image has been attached to her today, I rather think Medusa, whom Athena slighted, better represents feminine wisdom.

A pregnancy is not brought about by a woman alone, and it is unfair that only a woman has to face abortion. That is, it is the woman—not the man—who is injured by it. In a sense, abortion symbolizes the actual relationship between a man and a woman in that it is an experience that can break a woman's spirit and cause her to abandon her creativity. As Hillman suggests, to kill an unborn child is to lose hope for the future.

The Problem of Being a Victim

Trauma is discussed a lot these days. Some people even criticize Freud, who, under duress, turned his trauma theory into a fantasy theory. That is, when a female patient talked about an incestuous episode in her childhood, Freud took it as a reality at first; later he came to consider it as a fantasy, which he believed derived from her repressed desire for her father. Some people who have experienced the calamities of war or natural disaster suffer from various symptoms of posttraumatic stress disorder (PTSD). Women who have been raped or sexually abused suffer from a similar affliction. Those who were sexually abused in their childhood often conceal this experience and develop a dissociative disorder. The most extreme cases are found in multiple personality disorder (MPD, or dissociative identity disorder [DID]). Many such cases have been reported in the United States in the past twenty years. Japan has seen fewer cases than the United States, but it is also not uncommon there.

In Europe, in the latter part of the nineteenth century there were many cases of women with hysteria, and one hundred years later there are numerous cases of women with a dissociative disorder. How can we understand these phenomena? In the Victorian age, women wore tight corsets and led restricted lives. Society required them to live according to men's ideal image of the feminine. In those days women had far fewer occasions than men did to develop their abilities. For example, Breuer's case "Anna O" seemed to be much more intelligent than her brother, but it was her brother who received a higher education. Most likely those women's concealed creativity cause them to suffer from the hysteric syndrome. But today's women have many more occasions for achievement. At least they face fewer outer obstacles to self-development. Therefore, we must wonder why so many women still suffer from MPD or DID.

Perhaps today's women are metaphorically corseted in that the mass media strongly encourage them to conform to an ideal feminine image. Women who exhibited hysteria made Freud turn his eyes to the unconscious. And what are we now learning from women with MPD?

Through the process of psychotherapy, a woman with MPD gradually recalls her lost memories and begins to talk about a terrible experience from her childhood. In many cases she has been sexually abused by her father. When a therapist listens to such a story, especially when the therapist is female, it is difficult for her to remain detached, and she may be caught up in countertransference. The therapist herself feels threatened by a story that relates the most abominable crime a man can ever commit against a woman. Moreover, the therapist often finds it difficult not to become overly involved with this client and her story.

In cases of daughter-father incest, the client is a victim who feels a strong hatred for her father as the perpetrator or offender; sometimes she even brings a lawsuit against him. But can she be happier by doing this? I do not believe so. Once a woman sees herself as a victim, she always blames the offender, and she cannot reflect on herself. If the offender is her father, to deny and reject him is to deny and reject a part of herself—as her father's daughter. Accordingly, she will never accept herself totally.

The key is to understand the hurtful trauma as best we can and utilize forgiveness, so that real healing can occur. The story of a girl's sexual abuse by her father can be explained by Kavaler-Adler's theory, which is presented in chapter 2. If a girl fails to have an I-thou relationship with her mother in the pre-Oedipal stage, she forms one with her father. However, this primordial relationship will be influenced by the next Oedipal stage, in which the inner image of her father becomes a kind of demon lover, and she becomes spellbound by him. Tragically, daughter-father incest often results. Of course, the problem that gives rise to this situation is a mother's inability to love and guide her child. I believe this happens because the lineage of feminine spirituality is blocked. If a mother does not have this heritage herself, she is dependent on others and cannot live her own life. Her unlived creativity makes her both hate and envy her daughter. Thus the daughter feels a black void inside her and tries to do everything she can in order to fill it. Or she seeks a kind of mainstay because she has lost her essential, supporting core. Thus she clings to her father and tries to do everything possible to please him. By doing this, she wins a victory over her mother, but it makes her feel guilty at the same time, so she tries to please her mother, too. As a result, the daughter becomes accustomed to behaving as other people expect and has no sense of inner security.

Unlike earlier instances of MPD in which only a few personalities were evidenced, MPD cases of the late-twentieth century characteristically exhibit numerous personalities appearing within the patient, as if every persona turns out to be a personality and as if many people that we normally see in our dreams come out in reality. Moreover, among those personalities are some who have opposite gender personalities. One of my analysands with this disorder once said, "I am original only in the dream. In the dream I know who I am." But about reality she said, "I made myself according to other people's expectations of me." For this woman, it seems that the reality and the dream were reversed. In reality she felt as if she were in a dream.

A woman who has experienced the trauma of incestuous sexual abuse in childhood is the ultimate victim in this patriarchal world. A father is the dirty offender, and an innocent little girl is the poor victim. What a deplorable situation! Everyone feels pity for the girl and condemns the father. Even in such a case, however, if the girl clings to being a victim, no solution is possible. A healing resolution is based on understanding and forgiveness, which allows for the death of the victim's self and the rebirth of the true creative and spiritual self.

The analysand whose case I cited earlier recalled her lost memories because one of her personalities, who was male, wrote all of the stories of her past in a novel. Accepting these facts was her first step in recovery. When she remembered what her father did to her, his image degenerated. Gradually she came to forgive him as a person, although she could not tolerate what he had done to her. She forgave her rejecting mother, too. She came to understand that each of her parents had been in such difficult straits in those days that they may have been somewhat insane. This was her second step, but it was still not enough. Then one day she remembered how terribly she herself had tortured her father. This memory disturbed her because, up until that time, she had believed that she had been the only victim. However, she then remembered that she had played a nasty trick on her father to intentionally hurt him. This recollection shocked and depressed her terribly. From the abyss of this desperation she finally found hope for the future.

In this case, the analysand had a male personality inside her, like a twin brother, who wrote me this message:

In olden times
When men and animals lived together on Earth
If he wanted, a man could become an animal
An animal could become a man

So one was sometimes a man, sometimes an animal
There was no difference between them
And we used the same language
All the words of that time were magic words
The man's head had a marvelous power
The words that came up by chance
Produced marvelous things
The words suddenly began to have life

. . .

No one could explain it
The world was just as it was.
Do not hurt the "Magic Words."[6]

Quoting the Inuits' oral tradition, this poetic message made me feel that integrity and wisdom existed in my analysand's deeper psyche, although she did yet not recognize them. This poem also helped me to understand how the woman's creative words were healing and reflected feminine spirituality.

Women who suffer from MPD in today's world show the ultimate image of a woman who denies herself in order to conform to the expectations of others. Feminine spirituality unites the different expectations, and when this does not work, a woman's personality might become divided into segments as if each persona is floating in the air. As a result, a woman's personality does not take root in the Earth. Of course, women with MPD have had to produce these personalities to survive in an unbearable situation. However, the lack of feminine spirituality drives them to that point in the first place. These are women who have lost their hands completely. Their different personalities must be considered as their potential personas, just like the people who appear in their dreams, so it is important to accept them. Above all, a therapist must not turn her eyes away from her own soul, which is trembling in the depth of her psyche.

I have the impression that the word "trauma" has become too commonplace recently. Living in this world entails personal pain to a greater or lesser degree. Of course, trauma results from unjust and unacceptable harm. Even the experience of birth is considered traumatic, yet thanks to it humans can become very complex creatures full of possibilities.[7]

The term "victim" is also too frequently used. This sense of being a victim is an excuse that women use not to be creative. The handless maiden is also the image of a victim. Women are regarded as weaker than men, so it is easy to consider oneself a victim. Certainly women cannot compete with men in physical strength. Moreover, men have controlled this society for a long time, and women have been in the socially weaker position. However, I believe women have another kind of strength that men do not have. It is strength that is rooted in the Earth, and it allows women to understand, have insight, and forgive. It is feminine spirituality.

Women in the twentieth century strived for equal footing with men. They trained themselves to think like men. Although they felt a little uneasy about it, they came to neglect their inner voices little by little. Consequently, they put their most important asset aside somewhere. We need to recover our creativity and feminine spirituality.

Hands Receiving the Gods' Will

In Christian iconography, God is often represented as a big hand appearing from among clouds in the sky. The hand symbolizes the works of the gods, and many people believe that sick people will be healed when the gods' hands touch them. In the temple of Asclepius (the Greek god of medicine), a sick person went to a temple and slept in a special room called an *abaton*. When Asclepius appeared in a dream and touched the diseased part of the dreamer with his hand, the person was healed.[8] In the New Testament, Jesus Christ healed many sick people by touching them with his hands.[9] In Japanese, "te-ate" ('touching by hands') means "treatment." So, from ancient times people have believed in the healing function of the hands. When the gods' hands touched people, miraculous recoveries were believed to occur.

One reason I consider hands as a symbol of feminine spirituality is their ability to function as a receiver of the gods' will. One image of feminine spirituality is that of an ancient shamaness who received a message from the gods and made it known to people; the hands work as highly sensitive antennae that capture messages from the universe. When we use our hands to make something, we often discover that unexpected things occur. Our hands may be receiving messages from this universe, which we put into form. This also connects us with the inner universe of our psyche.

Fukumi Shimura, a well-known Japanese artist who dyes silk threads with plant-derived colors, says, "I gratefully receive the blessing of nature" when she creates beautiful woven cloth. She further says, "When I weave at the loom, I often feel that my hands surely think. Hands choose the color before the brain thinks. Hands catch the rhythm. And in such a moment an unexpected harmony of colors appears. Does a brain of hands make this decision before a command from the brain reaches the hands? No, it is not that way. It seems that the command comes from somewhere beyond the fingertips. Maybe it sounds a little strange, but seemingly there is another hand beyond the hand. A dancer once said that it is not the real hands, but these unseen hands that dance. But the real hands have to grasp them firmly and securely. It is amazing that the movement of hands is so delicate, subtle, and at the same time strong. And their touch is superior to the cosmic sensor."[10]

Our hands must always be ready to receive signals from the universe. If we do not try to do our best with our hands, those signals will pass us by. Shimura uses the expression "Shinbo-shutui" ("When there is an earnest wish, the hands follow it") and says that if your mind is full of ideas, and your hands do not follow them, these ideas are nothing but momentary self-relief and are not genuine. I believe she wants to emphasize the importance of using our hands to help the ideas take a certain form. She continues, "Hands are relentless. My hands know my true Self more than myself knows. When they move more quickly than I supposed, or when they endure well, I feel that they make me awake. Hands which stay close to a creative person never fall apart. Such are hands which take sides with me without a word, hands which never betray me, hands which are frightening. I wonder if we can do such work. We cannot stop reaching out our hands for those hands."[11] In this way she severely questions herself. Maybe we have to awaken the wisdom of our hands by devotedly using them. If we do that, the gods will likely come down to our hands and guide us.

Today the whole world is connected to the Internet. We can easily obtain all sorts of information from around the world. Does this situation give us a wider perspective? Unfortunately, it doesn't always. Information seen on the screen of a personal computer tends to diminish the gravity of the matter. If we are not connected firmly to the Earth, this flood of information confuses people and inflates their ego. The more information that flies about in the air, the deeper in the Earth we need to take root. To do this, we should value the planting of seeds with our hands. It may be the case that we can acquire precious things only by using our hands.

In today's world it seems to me all the more important to think about feminine spirituality. It is an urgent issue for women, men, and our planet. If we dig down deeper and deeper into the Earth, we will find our common heritage. We will also find hope that people all over the world will someday understand each other.

Conclusion

When I first asked myself what gives a woman self-confidence and dignity without becoming masculine or conforming to the feminine image that men expect, I began to think of feminine spirituality. In Okinawa, women are regarded as having a spiritual quality that men do not have, and for this reason men respect them. In the ancient world women must have had a certain authority, thanks to this feminine quality. However, since the patriarchal world took over, this feminine quality has been neglected and ultimately rejected. Nevertheless, some part of it continued to be transmitted from mothers to daughters for quite some time. Gradually this stream of spiritual groundwater tapered off, and today it has almost dried up. Today women have become nonchalant about metaphorically cutting off certain parts of their bodies in order to reshape themselves in the feminine framework that men expect. In the masculine world, women have buried their feminine spirituality in the depth of their psyches, and they do not even know exactly what it is anymore.

Therefore, I use hands as a symbol of feminine spirituality in order to give you a certain image to keep in mind. By this, I want to show that the loss of feminine spirituality damages women as seriously as literally cutting off their hands would do.

What can women do, then, to recover their lost hands? The first thing is to believe that feminine spirituality most certainly existed in the past and that it still exists somewhere deep in our soul—in old memories. In order to recall these ancient memories, women need to be creative. To be creative, women need to use their hands. No matter what people say, just let your hands move. Maybe in your writing or drawing or in any other thing you may make or do, you will find something substantial that helps you believe in yourself.

What emerges from the depth of your psyche is not always favorable and bright. You also need to accept the dark and frightening parts of yourself. This is because feminine wisdom works only when you accept both aspects. You need to find these various parts in yourself and be responsible for them. To recover feminine spirituality it is also necessary to find a way in which a man and a woman can be equal, for this constellates the brother-sister archetype. In such a relationship, a man and a woman accept their differences and respect each other, but neither one is under the other's domination. I believe this constitutes another type of hope for the future.

Finally, I would like to refer you to a series of drawings that a young woman artist produced. She had a dream, and the dream developed into these drawings, to which she added some words. The color photo gallery in this book shows these images and words by Mari Watanabe. Her drawings were displayed at an exposition of works by graduates of Tama Art University.

Just put your hands on your ears and close your eyes—then you might hear the sound of a waterfall.

> In nature the resolution of opposites is always an energic process: she acts symbolically in the truest sense of the word, doing something that expresses both sides, just as a waterfall visibly mediates between above and below. The waterfall itself is then the incommensurable third.
>
> —C. G. Jung, *Mysterium Coniunctionis*

I would like all of us to believe in our hands.

Notes

Introduction

1. In his newspaper column, cultural historian Shozaburo Kimura says that we should not overestimate the brain's direction, referring to a presentation by French psychophysiologist Jean François Lambert at the "Science and Sensibility" symposium held in Paris on June 18, 1994. There Lambert demonstrated that a pinprick on a fingertip is immediately transmitted as a signal to a specific point within the brain and that we feel this as pain almost instantly. However, when the signal is given directly to this part of the brain, a tiny bit of time elapses before we feel pain at the fingertip. Kimura points out possibilities of the wisdom of hands (Nihon Keizai Shimbun, evening edition, April 18, 1997).
2. R. Descartes, *Discourse de la méthode* (Paris: Librio, 1999), p. 44.
3. B. Ehrenreich and D. *English, Witches, Midwives, and Nurses: A History of Women Healers.*
4. E. Begg, *The Cult of the Black Virgin.*
5. S. Toyoda, *The Lineage of Feminine Spirituality*, pp. 63–69.
6. Toyoda, "The Unhappy Relationship with the Inner Woman," pp. 125–42.

Chapter 1

1. S. Freud, "Das Motiv der Kastchenwahl," p. 283; E. Erikson, "The Inner and Outer Space: Reflections on Womanhood," *Daedalus* 93 (1964): 582–97. Translated as "Josei to Naiteki Kuukan" in *Aidenthithi: Seinen to Kiki*, pp. 369–415.
2. M. Woodman, *Addiction to Perfection: The Still Unravished Bride.* Woodman discusses this theme in her other books as well; H. Barz, *For Men, Too: A Graceful Critique of Feminism*; J. Hillman, *Anima: An Anatomy of a Personified Notion.*
3. L. Freeman, *The Story of Anna O: The Woman Who Led Freud to Psychoanalysis.*

4. H. Dieckmann, *Gelebte Märchen: Lieblingsmärchen der Kindheit*, p. 180.

5. J. M. Ellis, *One Fairy Story Too Many: The Brothers Grimm and Their Tales*, pp. 130–31.

6. C. G. Jung, "Die psychologische Aspekte des Mutter-Archetypus," 9:i, para. 182.

7. M-L. von Franz, *Problems of the Feminine in Fairytales*, pp. 70–93; Dieckmann, *Gelebte Märchen*, pp. 174–96; C. P. Estés, *Women Who Run with the Wolves: Myths and Stories of the Wild Woman Archetype*, pp. 443–521; H. Kawai, *The Japanese Psyche: Major Motifs in the Fairy Tales of Japan*, pp. 125–42; T. Oda, *Mukashibanashi to Yumebunseki [Old Stories and Dream Analysis]*, pp. 205–224.

8. Von Franz, *Problems of the Feminine*, p. 86.

9. The only English-language book on this theme is W. P. Lebra's *Okinawan Religion: Belief, Ritual, and Social Structure*.

Chapter 2

1. T. Yokoo, *Mierumono to Mienaimono* [The Visible and the Invisible], p. 200.

2. P. Claudel, "Camille Claudel: Sculptor," in R-M. Paris, *Camille Claudel 1864–1943*. Translated by I. Nada and Y. Miyazaki as "Camille Claudel, choukokuka," pp. 13–14. This article originally appeared in the journal *L'Occident* (1905); it now appears in P. Claudel, *Oeuvres en prose* (Paris: Gallimard, 1965).

3. Toyoda, *The Lineage of Feminine Spirituality*, pp. 26–42.

4. P. Claudel, "Ma soeur Camille." Foreword in the catalogue for Rodin's 1951 exposition of Camille's works. In J. Cassar's *Dossier Camille Claudel*, it is found on pp. 391–99. It also appears as "Camille Claudel" in Claudel, *L'Oeil écoute*, pp. 250–59.

5. M. Woodman, *Addiction to Perfection: The Still Unravished Bride* and *The Pregnant Virgin: A Process of Psychological Transformation*.

6. S. Kavaler-Adler, *The Compulsion to Create: A Psychoanalytic Study of Women Artists*.

7. Kavaler-Adler, *The Creative Mystique: From Red Shoes Frenzy to Love and Creativity*, pp. 49–78.

8. Claudel, "Ma soeur Camille," in Cassar, *Dossier Camille Claudel*, p. 394, and in Claudel, *L'Oeil écoute*, p. 254.

9. Rodin is quoted by M. Morhardt in "Mlle. Camille Claudel," in *Mercure de France* (March, 1898). His observation also occurs in Cassar, *Dossier Camille Claudel*, p. 412; Claudel in Cassar, *Dossier Camille Claudel*, p. 395, and in Claudel, *L'Oeil écoute*, p. 255.

10. G. Bouté, *Camille Claudel: le miroir et la nuit*, p. 140.

11. J. Fayard, foreword in Cassar, *Dossier Camille Claudel*, p. 23.

12. E. Neumann, *Kunst und schöpferisches Unbewusstes*, p. 53.

13. H. Herrera, *Frida: A Biography of Frida Kahlo*, p. 107.

14. Ibid., p. 266.

15. Ibid., pp. 254, 288.

16. Ibid., pp. 260–61.

17. R. Stein, *Incest and Human Love: The Betrayal of the Soul in Psychotherapy*, p. 119.

18. Ibid., 119, 120–21.

19. J. Beebe, *Integrity in Depth*.

20. E. Leach, *The Structural Analysis of the Bible*, pp. 59–124.

Chapter 3

1. D. Suzuki, *Nihonteki Reisei [Japanese Spirituality]*, p. 73.

2. Ibid., pp. 17, 98–99.

3. Ibid., p. 43.

4. Ibid., p. 117.

5. Ibid., p. 75.

6. Y. Haft-Pomrock, *Hands: Aspects of Opposition and Complementarity in Archetypal Chirology*, p. 29.

7. Ibid., p. 22.

8. S. Nakazawa, "Doruido: Musuko niyoru Syukyo" [Druid: Religion by Sons], in S. Nakazawa, M. Turuoka, and K. Tukikawa, eds., *Keruto no Shukyo: Doruidizumu* [The Celtic Religion: Druidism], p. 112.

9. T. Kamata, *Shukyo to Reisei* [Religion and Spirituality], pp. 24–27.

10. B. B. Koltuv, *The Book of Lilith*.

11. Begg, *Cult of the Black Virgin*, pp. 97–102. Begg also presents numerous resources on the origin of the Black Virgin.

12. T. Mato, *The Black Madonna Within: Drawings, Dreams, Reflections*.

13. Lao Tzu, *Tao Te Ching*, pp. 3, 8; M. Yanagi, *Kuroi Seibo* [The Black Madonna], p. 47.

14. T. Yamaori, *Kindai Nihonjin no Biisiki* [The Aesthetic Senses of Modern Japanese People], p. 192.

15. A. Sexton, *The Complete Poems*, p. 421.

16. J-C. Schmitt, *La raison des gestes dans l'Occident médiéval*, Japanese translation, p. 63.

17. P. Quignard, *Le nom sur le bout de la langue*, Japanese translation, p. 101.

18. C. G. Jung, commentary on *The Secret of the Golden Flower*, in *Collected Works*, vol. 13, para. 22.

Chapter 4

1. Estés, *Women Who Run with the Wolves*, pp. 7, 343.
2. Hillman, *The Myth of Analysis: Three Essays in Archetypal Psychology*, p. 292.
3. E. Pattis Zoja, *Abortion: Loss and Renewal in the Search for Identity*.
4. Hillman, *Loose Ends: Primary Papers in Archetypal Psychology*, p. 39.
5. D. Tacy, *Remaking Men: Jung, Spirituality, and Social Change*.
6. H. Kanaseki, *Mahou-no-Kotoba* [Magic Words].
7. O. Rank, *The Trauma of Birth*.
8. K. Kerényi, *Der göttliche Arzt: Studien über Asklepios und seine Kultstatten*.
9. S. Tachikawa, *Kami no Te, Hito no Te: Gyakko no igakushi* [Divine Hand, Human Hand: The Other Side of the History of Medicine].
10. F. Shimura, *Hahanaru Iro* [The Color of Mother], pp. 119–20.
11. Ibid., p. 121.

Bibliography

Aeba, Takao. *Chi no Rekishigaku* [Historical Studies of Wisdom]. Tokyo: Shinchosha, 1997.

Ankori, Gannit. *Imaging Her Selves: Frida Kahlo's Poetics of Identity and Fragmentation*. Westport, Conn., and London: Greenwood, 2002.

Barz, Helmut. *For Men, Too: A Graceful Critique of Feminism*. Wilmette, Ill.: Chiron, 1990.

Beebe, John. *Integrity in Depth*. College Station: Texas A&M University Press, 1992.

Begg, Ean. *The Cult of the Black Virgin*. London: Arkana, 1985.

Bonvin, Jacques. *Vierges noires: la réponse vient de la terre*. Paris: Dervy, 1988.

Bouté, Gérard. *Camille Claudel: le miroir et la nuit: essai sur l'art de Camille Claudel*. Paris: Éditions de l'Amateur et des Catalogues raisonnés, 1995.

Cassar, Jacques. *Dossier Camille Claudel*. Paris: Librairie Séguier/Archimbaud, 1987.

Claudel, Paul. *L'oeil écoute: la peinture hollandaise, la peinture espagnole, écrit sur l'art*. Paris: Gallimard, 1964.

Daihourin, ed. *Jizo Sama Nyumon* [An Introduction to Zijo]. Tokyo: Daihourin-kaku, 1984.

———, ed. *Junrei/Henro: Kokoro to Rekishi* [The Pilgrimage: Essence and Tradition]. Tokyo: Daihourin-kaku, 1997.

———, ed. *Kannon Sama Nyumon* [An Introduction to Kannon]. Tokyo: Daihourin-kaku, 1981.

Delbée, Anne. *Une femme*. Paris: Presses de la Renaissance, 1982.

Dieckmann, Hans. *Gelebte Märchen: Lieblingsmärchen der Kindheit* [Lived Fairy Tales: Favorite Fairy Tales of Childhood]. Wilmette, Ill.: Chiron, 1986. Translated as *Otogibanashi wo Ikiru Hitotachi*. Osaka: Sougensya, 1992.

Ehrenreich, Barbara, and Deirdre English. *Witches, Midwives, and Nurses: A History of Women Healers.* New York: Feminist Press, 1973. Trans. H. Nagase as *Majo, Sanba, Kangohu.* Tokyo: Hosei University Press, 1996.

Ellis, John M. *One Fairy Story Too Many: The Brothers Grimm and Their Tales.* Chicago: University of Chicago Press, 1983. Trans. K. Ikeda and T. Satuma as *Hitotu Yokeina Otogibanashi.* Tokyo: Shinyosha, 1993.

Erikson, Erik H. *Identity: Youth and Crisis.* New York: W. W. Norton, 1968. Trans. N. Iwase as *Aidenthithi: Seinen to Kiki.* Tokyo: Kanazawa Bunko, 1973.

Estés, Clarissa Pinkola. *Women Who Run with the Wolves: Myths and Stories of the Wild Woman Archetype.* New York: Ballantine, 1992.

Freeman, Lucy. *The Story of Anna O: The Woman Who Led Freud to Psychoanalysis.* Northvale, N.J., and London: Jason Aronson, 1972.

Freud, Sigmund. "Das Motiv der Kastchenwahl." In *Gesammelte Werke,* vol. 10. Frankfurt am Main: S. Fischer Verlag, 1968. Trans. Y. Takahashi as "Kobakoerabi no motiifu," vol. 3. Kyoto: Jinbunshoin, 1969.

Fujiwara, Shigekazu. *Iyasi no Chikeigaku* [The Geomorphology of Healing]. Kyoto: Houzoukan, 1999.

Garrard, Mary D. *Artemisia Gentileschi.* Princeton: Princeton University Press, 1991.

Haft-Pomrock, Yael. *Hands: Aspects of Opposition and Complementarity in Archetypal Chirology.* Einsiedeln, Switzerland: Daimon, 1992.

Herrera, Hayden. *Frida: A Biography of Frida Kahlo.* New York: Harper and Row, 1983.

———. *Frida Kahlo: The Paintings.* Harper Collins, 1991.

Hillman, James. *Anima: An Anatomy of a Personified Notion.* Dallas: Spring Publications, 1985.

———. *Loose Ends: Primary Papers in Archetypal Psychology.* Dallas: Spring Publications, 1975.

———. *The Myth of Analysis: Three Essays in Archetypal Psychology.* New York: Harper and Row, 1972.

Horio, Makiko. *Frida Kahlo: Hikisakareta Jigazo* [Frida Kahlo: Torn-off Self-Portraits]. Tokyo: Chuo Koronsha, 1999.

Hurwitz, Siegmund. *Lilith, the First Eve: Historical and Psychological Aspects of the Dark Feminine.* Einsiedeln, Switzerland: Daimon, 1992.

Jung, C. G. Commentary on *The Secret of the Golden Flower.* Zurich: Rascher, 1957. In the *Collected Works,* vol. 13. London: Routledge and Kegan Paul, 1968.

———. *Mysterium Coniunctionis.* Zurich: Rascher, 1955. In the *Collected Works,* vol. 14. London: Routledge and Kegan Paul, 1963.

————. "Die psychologische Aspekte des Mutter-Archetypus" [Psychological Aspects of the Mother Archetype]. From *Von den Wurzeln des Bewusstseins.* Zurich: Rascher, 1954. In the *Collected Works,* vol. 9. London: Routledge and Kegan Paul, 1959.

————. "Die transzendente Funktion" [The Transcendent Function]. Unpublished ms., 1916; later published in *Geist und Werk.* Zurich: Rhein, 1958. In the *Collected Works,* vol. 8. London: Routledge and Kegan Paul, 1960.

Kahlo, Frida. *The Diary of Frida Kahlo: An Intimate Self-Portrait.* Introduction by Carlos Fuentes. New York: Abradale, 1995.

Kamata, Toji. *Shukyo to Reisei* [Religion and Spirituality.] Tokyo: Kadokawa Shobo, 1995.

Kanaseki, Hisao, trans. *Mahou-no-Kotoba* [Magic Words] (Inuits' oral tradition); illus. Samito Yunoki. Tokyo: Hukuinkan, 1993.

Kavaler-Adler, Susan. *The Compulsion to Create: A Psychoanalytic Study of Women Artists.* New York and London: Routledge, 1993.

————. *The Creative Mystique: From Red Shoes Frenzy to Love and Creativity.* New York and London: Routledge, 1996.

Kawai, Hayao. *The Japanese Psyche: Major Motifs in the Fairy Tales of Japan.* Dallas: Spring Publications, 1988.

Kerényi, Karl. *Der göttliche Arzt: Studien über Asklepios und seine Kultstatten.* Trans. M. Okada as *Ishin Asukurepiosu.* Tokyo: Hakusuisya, 1997.

Koltuv, Barbara Black. *The Book of Lilith.* York Beach, Me.: Nocolas-Hays, 1986.

Lao Tzu. *Tao Te Ching.* Trans. D. Hinton. Washington, D.C.: Counterpoint, 2000.

Le Clézio, J. M. G. *Diego et Frida.* Paris: Stock, 1993.

Leach, Edmond. *The Structural Analysis of the Bible.* Trans. S. Suzuki as *Seisyo no Kouzou Bunseki.* Tokyo: Kinokuniya, 1990.

Lebra, William P. *Okinawan Religion: Belief, Ritual, and Social Structure.* Honolulu: University of Hawaii Press, 1966.

Lindauer, Margaret A. *Devouring Frida: The Art History and Popular Celebrity of Frida Kahlo.* Hanover and London: Wesleyan University Press, 1999. Also published by University Press of New England, 1999.

Mato, Tataya. *The Black Madonna Within: Drawings, Dreams, Reflections.* Chicago and LaSalle, Ill.: Open Court, 1994.

Mochizuki, Shinjo. *Zijo Bosatu.* Tokyo: Gakuseisya, 1989.

Nakazawa S., M. Turuoka, and K. Tukikawa, eds. *Keruto no Shukyo: Doruidizumu* [The Celtic Religion: Druidism]. Tokyo: Iwanami Shoten, 1997.

Neumann, Erich. *Kunst und schöpferisches Unbewusstes.* Zürich: Rascher, 1954. Trans. H. Ujihara and M. Nomura as *Geijutu to Souzouteki Muisiki.* Osaka: Sougensya, 1984.

Oda, Takao. *Mukasibanasi to Yumebunseki* [Old Stories and Dream Analysis]. Osaka: Sougensya, 1993.

Ogawa, Kozo, Kocho Nishimura, Kyotaro Nishikawa, Takayuki Yamazaki, and Shoen Endo. *Senju Kannon.* Tokyo: Mainichi Shinbunsya, 1986.

Paris, Reine-Marie. *Camille Claudel 1864–1943.* Paris: Gallimard, 1984.

Pattis Zoja, Eva. *Abortion: Loss and Renewal in the Search for Identity.* London and New York: Routledge, 1997.

Paz, Octavio. *El laberinto de la soledad.* Mexico: Fondo de Cultura Economica, 1950. Trans. T. Takayama and A. Kumagai as *Kodoku no Meikyu.* Tokyo: Housei University Press, 1982.

Quignard, Pascal. *Le nom sur le bout de la langue.* Paris: Gallimard,1995. Trans. K. Takahasi as *Shita no Saki made Dekakatta Namae.* Tokyo: Seidosya, 1998.

Rank, Otto. *The Trauma of Birth.* New York: Dover, 1993.

Rivera, Diego. *My Art, My Life: An Autobiography.* With Gladys March. New York: Dover, 1991.

Schmitt, Jean-Claude. *La raison des gestes dans l'Occident médiéval.* Paris: Gallimard, 1990. Trans. T. Muramatu as *Chusei no Miburi.* Tokyo: Misuzu Shobo, 1996.

Schmoll gen. Eisenwerth, J. Adolf. *Auguste Rodin and Camille Claudel.* Munich and New York: Prestel, 1994.

Sexton, Anne. *The Complete Poems.* New York: Mariner, 1999.

Shimura, Fukumi. *Hahanaru Iro* [The Color of Mother]. Tokyo: Kyuryu Do, 1999.

Stein, Robert. *Incest and Human Love: The Betrayal of the Soul in Psychotherapy.* Baltimore: Penguin, 1974.

Suzuki, Daisetz. *Nihonteki Reisei.* Tokyo: Iwanami, 1972. Trans. N. Waddell as *Japanese Spirituality.* Tokyo: Japan Society for the Promotion of Science, 1972.

Tachikawa, Shoji. *Kami no Te, Hito no Te: Gyakko no igakushi* [Divine Hand, Human Hand: The Other Side of the History of Medicine]. Kyoto: Jinbun Shobo, 1995.

Tacy, David J. *Remaking Men: Jung, Spirituality, and Social Change.* London and New York: Routledge, 1997.

Tanaka, Hitohiko. *Kuro Maria no Nazo* [The Mystery of the Black Virgin]. Tokyo: Iwanami Shoten, 1993.

Tibol, Raquel. *Frida Kahlo: An Open Life.* Albuquerque: University of New Mexico Press, 1993.

Toyoda, Sonoko. "The Lineage of Feminine Spirituality." Diploma thesis, C. G. Jung Institute, Zurich, 1992.

———. "The Unhappy Relationship with the Inner Woman." In *Kyodo kenkyu danseiron* [Discussions of the Males], ed. Y. Nishikawa and M. Ogino, 125–42. Kyoto: Jinbun Shoin, 1999.

Trillat, Etienne. *Histoire de l'histérie*. Paris: Seghers, 1986. Trans. I. Yasuda and R. Yokokura as *Hisuteri no Rekisi*. Tokyo: Seidosya, 1998.

Ueyama, Yasutoshi. *Majo to Kirisuto-kyo* [Witches and Christianity]. Kyoto: Jinbun Shoin, 1993.

Von Franz, Marie-Louise. *Problems of the Feminine in Fairytales*. Dallas: Spring Publications, 1972.

Watanabe, Moriaki. *Paul Claudel: Gekiteki Souzouryoku no Sekai* [Paul Claudel: The World of Dramatic Imagination]. Tokyo: Chuou Kouron Sha, 1975.

Woodman, Marion. *Addiction to Perfection: The Still Unravished Bride*. Toronto: Inner City Books, 1982.

———. *The Pregnant Virgin: A Process of Psychological Transformation*. Toronto: Inner City Books, 1985.

Yamaori, Tetsuo. *Kindai Nihonjin no Biisiki* [The Aesthetic Senses of Modern Japanese People]. Tokyo: Iwanami Shoten, 2001.

Yanagi, Munemoto. *Kuroi Seibo* [The Black Madonna]. Tokyo: Hukutake Shoten, 1986.

Yanagida, Kunio. "Imo no Chikara" [The Sister's Power]. In *Complete Works*, vol. 11. Tokyo: Chikuma Shobo, 1990.

Yasuda, Yoshinori. *Daichi Boshin no Jidai* [The Age of Earth Mother Goddess]. Tokyo: Kadokawa Shoten, 1991.

Yokoo, Tadanori. *Mierumono to Mienaimono* [The Visible and the Invisible]. Tokyo: Chikumashobo, 1992.

Yunohara, Kanoko. *Camille Claudel*. Tokyo: Asahi-Shinbunsya, 1988; in Japanese.

Zamora, Martha. *Frida Kahlo: The Brush of Anguish*. San Francisco: Chronicle, 1991.

Index

Page numbers in *italic* typeface refer to illustrations.

and limitations on feminine spirituality, 94–98; stepmother archetype as destroyer of feminine wisdom, 21, 22, 25; and women's derivative power from men, 26; and women's self-worth, 14–15. *See also* children; mother-daughter relationship

Medusa, 5, 44, 112

Memory (Kahlo), 59, *61*

men: dependence on women's maternal function, 94–95; fears of feminine wisdom, 5, 9, 20–21, 25, 103; focus on concrete objects, 100; insensitivity of, 58, 63; loss of feminine spirituality in individuation, 112; reliance of women on, 26, 36, 56, 58, 105–106, 114; suppression of feminine creativity, 14, 20–21, 25, 105; value of feminine spirituality for, 42, 44, 75–76, 108; women as guardian spirits of, 32. *See also* masculine values

mental disorders and suppression of feminine creativity, 14, 30–31, 104, 113–15, 116

mercy and compassion, hands as symbolic of, 89–90. *See also* Virgin Mary

Merlet, Agnes, 37

mind/body dualism, 3–5

Miriam, Hebrew prophetess, 72

Mona Lisa (Da Vinci), 52–53

Montserrat, Black Virgin of, 79, 80, *82*

mother-daughter relationship: artistic search for mother, 60, 67; and failure to pass on feminine spirituality, 104; inherent inequality of, 72; as negative influence for artists, 36,

38, 54–56, 58, 68; and spiritual void for women, 48, 49, 114

Mother Earth goddess, scope of feminine powers, 79, 86, 96

motherhood. *See* maternity

multiple personality disorder (MPD), 113–15, 116

Murasaki-Shikibu, 105

My Birth (Kahlo), 58

My Nurse and I (Kahlo), 60, *62*

"My Sister Camille" (Claudel, P.), 46–47

mythology: and Claudel's creativity, 44–46; couple vs. sister-brother relationships, 43–44; and triumph of masculine power, 5–6, 112; and women as active, 12–13, 79, 86. *See also* religion

nature: Japanese spiritual connection to, 73–74, 75, 78, 88; and Kannon worship, 88, 92; loss of human connection to, 4, 9; as sustainer of feminine spirituality, 23, 29, 31, 107–108; and traditional cultures, 32, 78, 79

Neumann, Erich, 52–53

Niobe, 44–46

nyori, 87

object-relation theory, 48

Oda, Takao, 30–31

Okinawa, feminine spirituality in, 31–32, 106

pain and suffering: as response to spiritual void, 62–63, 67–69, 112–17; and victimhood, 37, 68, 112–17

ISBN 1-58544-435-9